By One Vote

CAROLE EGLASH-KOSOFF

By One Vote

by

CAROLE EGLASH-KOSOFF

Published by

Valley Village Publishing

www.ValleyVillagePublishing.com

By One Vote Copyright © 2012 Carole Eglash-Kosoff
Cover Design and Illustration by: Jon C Jackson
For more information contact Valley Village publishing at
info@valleyvillagepublishing.com
Phone   818 762 8190
Website: www.byonevote-thebook.com
10-Digit ISBN: 0983960135 (e-book)
13-Digit ISBN: 978-0-9839601-3-3 (e-book)

10-Digit ISBN: 0983960127 (Softcover)
13-Digit ISBN: 978-0-9839601-2-6 (Softcover)
Printed in the United States of America

Also by Carole Eglash-Kosoff

The Human Spirit
~ Apartheid's Unheralded Heroes

When Stars Align

Winds of Change

Dedication

This book is dedicated to history's unsung heroes... those men and women whose convictions altered the direction of our society. Social justice moves slowly and unevenly... but it does move, sometimes by one vote!

The Law of Unintended Consequences

For want of a nail the shoe was lost.
For want of a shoe the horse was lost.
For want of a horse the rider was lost.
For want of a rider the battle was lost.
For want of a battle the kingdom was lost.
And all for the want of a horseshoe nail.

PROLOGUE

One vote…the decision of a single individual, has altered the direction of our country on numerous occasions. Sometimes it has moved our entire nation further into the dark but often it has moved us in the direction of curing inequities that had evolved through decades of history.

We live in a period of economic and political unrest and we believe it to be worse than at any time in our history…but it may not be! America's two hundred plus years of existence has been one of turmoil, dissension, and war. It has been a time of alternating economic growth and stagnation. Each decade has found stalwarts and dissenters convinced that they, alone, have the best solution for the country's ills.

A surprising number of events that altered the country's direction resulted from the vote of a single individual either in support of a change or opposed to it. Names such as James Bayard, Edmund Ross, and Joseph Bradley are unknown, but during their lifetimes, they altered the fabric or our nation as significantly as Americans whose names are more famous. This book, *By One Vote*, tells these stories. The events are factual; the dramatizations surrounding them are the studied imagination of the author.

The Butterfly Effect:

A unique decision by a single individual can produce a *'butterfly effect'* whereby a small change at one place or point in time can result in large unpredicted differences at a later time.

TABLE OF CONTENTS

I

ESTABLISHING THE NATION'S CAPITOL

The war for independence had been fought and won. In 1783, in a most unlikely turn of events, General George Washington's army trapped the main British force, led by General Lord Cornwallis, on the peninsula at Yorktown Heights. French ships, eager to help any country who would fight their traditional enemy, had kept the waiting British ships at bay and their Captains frustrated, unable to anchor and extricate their embattled Redcoats. The British forces were forced to surrender, and although there were still thousands of British soldiers spread through the colonies and another covey of ships flying the Union Jack in Charleston, the war was over. Three thousand miles to the east, in London, King George III and the Parliament heaped blame on one another. A ripe plum of the British Empire had been lost due to sheer incompetence. Unpaid soldiers, a bankrupt treasury, and men from thirteen colonies with widely diverse interests, and spread more than a thousand miles along the Atlantic seaboard, had held together long enough to defeat the 18th century's most dominant world power.

There would now be a new country to govern. The First Continental Congress had given way to the Second Continental Congress. With independence now a reality, those men had turned over the leadership of the country to

1

the Congress of the Confederation. The task of this new group would be to get a Constitution approved, a President chosen, and determine whether a Parliamentary or Congressional form of government would be established. This new 'gathering' had little power and, without the external threat of the war that had unified the colonies, it was difficult to even amass a quorum to function. Differences and dissension among the thirteen separate colonies was already beginning to gel.

Delegates from around the country milled around, greeting old friends, in the minimally furnished room of the Pennsylvania State House on a humid April day. Samuel Huntington, one of Connecticut's leading citizens, and a signer of the Declaration of Independence, banged his gavel. It took several minutes for the men to find their seats. Late comers were still straggling in. Others found the heat oppressive and began removing jackets.

Huntington's patience was wearing. They were already more than an hour late in starting their session.

"Can we have order?" he said in a normal speaking voice. "Gentlemen," he said, his voice raised several notches. "We are already convening an hour late and we need to discuss the pressing matter of our debt."

"Mr. Huntington...Mr. Chairman," Thomas McKean of Delaware, stood, his arm raised for recognition. "I don't believe we have a quorum. We can chat and we can debate until June but it is doubtful we can ever get our friends from all thirteen colonies to agree. We can't even agree on where to eat our meals or when to take a piss."

"Please, Mr. McKean," Huntington pleaded. "The Chair recognizes the gentleman from Rhode Island."

"Why," another delegate shouted. "Does he need to take a piss?"

Samuel Huntington glared at the speaker from South Carolina, but said nothing.

"I'll hold my water for now, Mr. Chairman, if my outspoken friend will hold his tongue. Rhode Island will not support the proposed 5% levy on imports."

"In other words," the South Carolinian laughed, "You'll piss on it."

Snickers filled the room and even Huntington was forced to smile.

"Let's just say that my enthusiasm for such a levy has been heavily dampened."

"Hear...hear," the delegates roared. It would take more than good humor to resolve the financing dilemma, however.

"Gentlemen," Huntington, smiled, banging his gavel, and trying to restore order. "Gentlemen, at the present time we are even unable to pay the accumulated interest on what we owe. Let me remind you of the magnitude of the problem. We owe more than $40 million and we have approved no sources of revenue to repay these obligations. Twenty percent of it is owed to the French and Dutch. These countries were happy to support us during our scuffle with the British. They disliked England and understood we had the resources to repay the money. The balance of the money owing is government bonds and continental certificates that have been purchased by American citizens. These certificates were issued by

military officers in order to purchase, or impress supplies, and to pay soldiers and officers over the past battle-weary years.

"To pay the interest and reduce the debt, the Continental Congress...of which some of you were members, twice proposed an amendment to the Articles granting them the power to impose a 5% duty on imports, but such amendments required the consent of all thirteen states. The gentlemen from Rhode Island and Virginia, fearing for the stability of their fledgling mercantile interests, rejected the 1781 imposition of duties. Meanwhile, the delegates from New York, on advice of banking interests in their state, rejected a revised plan submitted two years later.

"Without revenue," Huntington continued, "We are not able to even pay the interest on our outstanding debt. And, most of your states, meanwhile, have consistently failed, or openly refused, to meet the requisitions for funds requested of them by the Continental Congress. Those problems, still unresolved, have now been turned over to us. We must resolve them.   Everyone understands that each colony accumulated its own debts and is struggling to meet them. There may also be a growing anti-Federalist sentiment throughout the country and a continuing suspicion against centralized authority that would usurp a state's ability to control its own affairs."

"Mr. Chairman," Henry Laurens, the undisciplined representative from South Carolina, stood.   "All pissing aside, the largest portion of the debt to which you refer was accumulated by the northern states and these states are eager to have our new government assume their burden."

"Mr. Laurens," Huntington said, unwilling to recognize others wishing to be heard.   "That is where our struggles against the British were the heaviest.   You cannot have already forgotten Bunker Hill and Valley Forge."

"I have not forgotten, Mr. Chairman, but you are asking those of us from the south, and our rural brethren, to take on a heavy burden. If our Congress assumes this debt, our states would share in that obligation without assurances that levies passed would not cripple us. Ask my esteemed colleague, Mr. Peyton Randolph of Virginia…has not his state already paid off most of what it borrowed during the war?"

Randolph nodded. "We have, and our taxpayers should not be assessed again to bail out those states that were less prudent in their finances. Furthermore, I believe the plan as recommended is far beyond the scope of our new national government."

*****

Two hundred miles to the south an entirely different conversation was proceeding.

"James, sit and share a glass of wine with me," Thomas Jefferson said as his close friend, James Madison, entered the small tavern across from the Virginia Assembly that had recently relocated to the central heart of Richmond. It now met in the same building that had housed the original House of Burgess, the colony's first legislative body. The war with the British had forced Virginia to move its state government from Williamsburg. The tall, gangly, red-haired, Jefferson, was seated, holding a wet cloth to the bump on his forehead. They were a odd looking pair when they stood next to one another. Jefferson, well over six feet tall, towered over his friend, more than a foot shorter. But their minds were as one, both intelligent...both steadfast in their desire to bend this new country into their Virginia-bred, democratic vision.

"Did you hit your head...again? You see, Thomas, there are occasional advantages to being short," Madison

laughed. "Innkeeper," he said, turning his head. "A glass of ale for me! If I drink wine this early in the day, it clouds my thoughts."

"These old taverns were built for short, portly British gentlemen...no offense meant," Jefferson lamented. "Every time I enter one I worry about hitting my head on a ceiling rafter. This time I wasn't paying attention. So, while my head may be cloudy, James, I have never known your thoughts to be anything but clear and concise. Now, let me tell you about the latest deviousness from our old nemesis, Alexander Hamilton."

Thomas Jefferson   **James Madison**

"What has he done to upset you this time?" Madison said, knowing the suave man from New York, who had the President's ear, was always filled with new ideas, most of which benefitted his wealthy friends from the mercantile north.

"Dear Alex is trying to persuade President Washington to use his influence to permanently situate our nation's capitol in New York or Philadelphia. He says every nation in Europe has always located its capitol in its largest city...London, Rome, Madrid...the center of commerce, and all that."

Madison laughed. "His timing is terrible and I certainly hope old George won't listen to him. Too many of us still remember the riots in Philadelphia in 1783 when angry army veterans demanded all the back pay they were due. The Congress was forced to flee to Princeton, New Jersey. A couple of them barely got out of their nightshirts. When Governor Dickenson was asked to call out the militia, he refused. It seems he thought the men had a valid complaint. Anyway, neither Virginia nor the rest of the states south of us will agree to locate the capital in New York or Philadelphia. If we're to set our capitol into a populated community, why not situate it in Richmond, or even Charleston?" Madison averred.

"It's because he understands, as well as you or I do, that any decision will bring considerable economic benefit to states that will about the new capitol. Our President knows the area around here. He loves Alexandria and it's close to his Mount Vernon home. Actually it should make no difference to him. He'll be long retired before the new site is developed although he may be able to see it from where he and Martha will likely be buried."

"The new Federal government must be on a site apart from the states. That is the only way to avoid becoming embroiled in the problems of a particular state," Madison said, pausing to take a sip from his newly arrived tankard. "Hamilton certainly does enjoy putting a burr under your saddle."

"I don't trust him," Jefferson said, standing to stretch his legs, careful to avoid hitting his head again. "I don't like the direction he wants our country to take. He'd have one large federal government and damn the states. He doesn't care for the rights of the individual at all if they conflict with the government. He'd be happy to make the common man subservient to the Federal government."

"I'm more worried about his plans to have the Federal government assume all war debts," Madison said in a more serious tone. "It isn't as if the Congress has access to any revenue. Our soldiers still have large sums of back pay due them. The Federal government would have to levy new taxes and that would give it even more power. Remember what William Pitt, England's Prime Minister, said a few years ago, 'Unlimited power is apt to corrupt the minds of those who possess it.' That would be the eventual result of too much centralized power. We need to remain a 'confederation' not a federation. Power should remain with the states."

"I believe Alexander's mind has been corrupted for far too long. Robert Morris's influence has besotted his thinking."

"I don't deny that Morris' money was useful during the war," Madison conceded. "If he had not served as Superintendent of Finance and used a great deal of his personal wealth, our soldiers would have had to fight with their hands instead of the arms he'd purchased. Remember, he financed the movement of General Washington's army from New York State to Yorktown. He acted as quartermaster for the trip and supplied over $1,400,000 from his personal funds and credit to feed and supply the Army.

I'm told he often took out loans from friends and risked his personal reputation by issuing notes on his own signature to purchase sorely needed military materiel. He did this during the same year that New Hampshire contributed only $3,000 worth of beef toward the war effort, and all the colonies combined contributed less than $800,000. " Madison said.

"I agree. Getting thirteen separately founded colonies to agree on anything isn't easy. I think many would just as soon be independent countries as part of any union. If that were to happen, I fear, European powers would gobble us up one at a time."

Robert Morris was born in England but moved to Maryland as a young man. He was bright, his family was well-connected and, by the time he left his teen years, he was well ensconced in the shipping business, moving goods, and slaves, between Great Britain and her colonies. He helped underwrite the sailing of the first American ship to China.

Robert Morris

"Leverage, my sons...leverage," he engrained in each of his five sons. "Use your capital wisely and it will return you tenfold. And it is that money that will buy you influence and the proper life."

He became active in 1765 when the English Parliament passed the onerous Stamp Act, imposing a tax on all legal documents.

His loyalty to Great Britain, his country of birth, was sorely tested as, more and more, the schism with the colonies deepened. By the time the war began, Morris sided with Pennsylvania and threw his financial support to help the underfunded Continental Army. He had been a signer of the Declaration of Independence, the Articles of Confederation, and the United States Constitution. He was a confidante of George Washington, and often thought of as 'the most powerful man in America or the sobriquet he preferred, 'Financier of the Revolution.'

In July 1776, Morris had actually voted against the Congressional motion for independence, causing the Pennsylvania delegation, which was split 4-3, to cast its vote against seceding from Great Britain. The following day, however, he agreed to abstain, allowing Pennsylvania to vote for independence. Two months later he signed the Declaration of Independence telling Benjamin Franklin "I am not one of those politicians that run testy when my own plans are not adopted. I think it is the duty of a good citizen to follow when he cannot lead."

*****

"Robert, I want you as my Secretary of the Treasury," George Washington said as soon as his election as the country's first President became official.

"Thank you for the honor, George… excuse me, Mr. President. Your new title is one I'll have to get used to. I would like nothing more than to accept your offer, but I must decline," the more than portly Morris said, sitting across from his old friend. "Most of the Congressmen from the South distrust me ever since I recommended taxing slaves. You need someone acceptable to all the colonies."

"Yes, I remember. That proposal wasn't too popular among our friends on South Carolina and Georgia," Washington smiled.

"Maybe not, but it would have brought in some much needed revenue to help you fight the war. Anyway, ever since, they've looked with suspicion on every suggestion I've made. You need someone less controversial. I'll be around to help if you need me but choose Hamilton. He's bright and understands what's necessary to put our country on a sound financial footing."

"I'm not sure Alexander is respected any better. He and Jefferson argue like two cats in heat. Still, I will follow your suggestion."

*****

Alexander Hamilton paced the room while his long time mentor, Robert Morris, read his *'1790 Report on the Public Credit.'*

"I'd like present it to President Washington and, with his approval, to the Congress," Hamilton said, confident in his report but nervous that this financial giant would find fault in it.

"It reads well, Alexander," Morris said, sitting back, folding his hands over his more than ample mid-section.

"It contains each of the seven points that are absolutely necessary to establish our new government on a firm financial footing. You did well."

Hamilton breathed a silent sigh of relief.

"Your first proposal is brief and cogent," Morris said, reading aloud. "All loans foreign governments had made to the United States during the Revolution will be repaid in full, along with accrued interest. The total, estimated at just over $10,000,000.00, will all be repaid through a combination of tax revenues and domestic borrowing. That's just fine.

"But your second recommendation is more controversial," he conceded, his broad forehead wrinkling. "All debts that the Continental Congresses has incurred by borrowing from American citizens and state governments are also to be repaid in full. This will include notes that were issued to pay the soldiers, farmers, and merchants who supplied our

revolutionary armies.   This debt is estimated to exceed
$40,000,000.00. All the various forms of borrowing are to be
exchanged for new federally issued bonds, payable at
favorable interest rates."

"This new form of bond will allow the Treasury to balance
our future financial obligations in an orderly fashion,"
Hamilton said, hopeful that his friend would concur.

"Perhaps," Morris said, "But…and it is a big 'but', let's not
ignore that my friends and I will benefit greatly from your
proposal and that fact will not be lost on those opposing your
program."

"That's true.   James Madison and his Jeffersonian
supporters will look with suspicion on anything I propose.
They believe that the federal government ought to negotiate
these domestic debts to less than their face value since, in
most cases, those who had first owned the securities have
already sold them."

"They're correct," Morris noted. "The inflation of the war
years and the depressed conditions of the 1780s forced many
of the original owners, including all the men who fought in
the war, to sell them at substantial losses. The speculators,
including many of my wealthy friends bought these deeply
discounted notes. They stand to reap huge windfall gains
under your redemption program. I'd make a considerable
profit as well if this program is adopted."

"If I can't get the first two proposals passed, my third and
final recommendation will be similarly doomed. I am

proposing that the federal government assume the still unpaid debts that each state government accumulated during the Revolution. The total of this debt exceeds $25,000,000.00."

"I don't wonder," Morris laughed. "Each state's effort to pay off their debts has varied greatly and you are now asking those states that have been fiscally diligent to subsidize the other states that ignored the problem. Mr. Jefferson will be distraught about the cumulative cost of assumption...more than $75,000,000.00 in a country with no federally sanctioned source of revenue. He would not have acquiesced to such recommendations if they had been made by someone whose motives he trusts and, you, Mr. Hamilton, do not fall into that category."

"I know. President Washington has not been shy about telling Mr. Jefferson and me how much he dislikes playing referee to his Secretary of State and Secretary of Treasury. His Cabinet meetings display our mutual dislike. Our hostility and vitriol have disrupted more than one meeting."

*****

"Hamilton is a chameleon," Jefferson had repeatedly told his friends. "One always has to look around the back of one of his proposals to see whose ass is being gored. Someone will always benefit from his programs, and too often it is his banking friends. I'm sure his friend, Morris, has his grubby profit-making hands in there somewhere. This 'assumption' plan of his is just another of his ploys to centralize the country's financial power in the Treasury Department...his department."

When Hamilton's plan was debated in Congress a month later, Jefferson and Madison had successfully convinced most of their southern associates to cast their votes against Hamilton's assumption plan to absorb state debts. Now, Hamilton, Morse, and their supporters were facing an unanticipated organized chorus objecting to each proposal. It was a contentious debate, testing already raw relationships.

Alexander Hamilton

"Profiteers!" "French lackeys!" "Go back to England...we didn't fight the British for you to make us just like them." Cooler heads kept the most bellicose from striking one another. Hamilton's fourth proposal dealt with taxation. Six months earlier he had convinced President Washington to enact a tariff, setting duties on imports, and designed to raise revenue for the new government. These duties failed to raise enough money and Hamilton was now forced to recommend a further increase in tariffs and the introduction of a new tax...an excise tax on distilled spirits.

James Monroe paced the room, his hands moving like windmills. He usually deferred to Mr. Jefferson or Mr.

Madison but this proposal was too much and he had lost his usual calm demeanor.

"This will be the first tax levied by the national government on a domestic product," he shouted, punctuating the air with his fist as Madison looked on, smiling at his young acolyte.

"He intends to assess any corn products that are converted to alcohol. He reasons that an excise on whiskey will be the least objectionable form of taxation the government can levy. He certainly doesn't understand human nature if he thinks people won't object to a tax on alcohol."

"Clever though," Madison acknowledged. "He's solicited the support of some social reformers, who hope that a 'sin tax' can raise public awareness about the harmful effects of alcohol."

"And all he got when the law was first passed was a four year rebellion by Pennsylvania's western farmers. Now he wants to try it again."

Hamilton would have preferred to establish a tax on property but he was warned that these taxes would be so ill-received that a public outcry was certain to take place. The states were already taxing both property and voting privileges, and they wanted no interference from the central government in that arena. His remaining proposals, the establishment of a national bank, the establishment of a mint to create a common coinage for the country, and the encouragement of programs to develop the country's manufacturing capability, would be voted on at a later date, once the smoke had cleared from adoption of the most critical financial issues.

Moving through the Congressional halls at the same time as Hamilton's fiscal programs was the Residence Act. This bill would establish a permanent location for the nation's capitol and, once again, there was conflict. Hamilton and his financial supporters proposed to keep it in New York where the current Congress was meeting. The large delegation from Virginia, led by Thomas Jefferson and James Madison, and supported by most of the southern delegations, preferred an area along the Potomac River in land that would be ceded by the states of Virginia and Maryland.

Fights and near brawls erupted in the taverns around Federal Hall, the former New York City Hall, and now the seat of the Confederation of the Congress as Federalists, a name adopted by supporters of Alexander Hamilton, argued with Democratic Republicans, the name adopted by followers of Thomas Jefferson. On a June afternoon, in the midst of increasing political discord, Alexander Hamilton and Robert Morris sat across from Thomas Jefferson and James Madison in a small private room at the Amsterdam tavern. The noise from the adjoining general bar and dining area ebbed and flowed but these four men were there to focus on important matters and they ignored the cacophony coming through the thin walls.

"Thomas, the country needs to adopt the financial recommendations I've submitted," Hamilton said to a stone-faced Jefferson, frustration in his voice. Negotiating with Thomas Jefferson was always acrimonious.

"I know you do, Hamilton, but we'll be damned if we will allow your friends to make a financial killing by accumulating every debt and throwing it into a federal cauldron you can stir like so much witch's brew," Jefferson retorted.

Federal building, New York City, 1790

"We're a country now, Mr. Jefferson," Morris interjected. "We need to think like a nation, rather than Virginians and Pennsylvanians."

"It's the Virginians and Pennsylvanians that are the reason we have a country," Madison said, "And not the other way around."

"If we don't have a strong central government, France or Great Britain will eventually swallow us up," Hamilton said, striding across the room.

"Thomas, you and I have differing visions on how our country should be governed and I doubt we will ever agree.

But, there must be a central government, if for no other reason than to confront the larger more powerful nations of the world and speak to them with a strong single voice. You, of all people who have lived and negotiated with England and France, should understand that. What do we have to do to get your support for my financial program? Robert and I have thought a great deal about it and we are prepared to lower the assumption amount from $25 million to $21 million. We will also add a clause that Virginia, having settled its own debts, will not be responsible for any of it."

Jefferson and Madison looked at one another. They had been in synch for years on their thinking and their desires for the country. It was a good offer and it would sway many of the undecided Senators.

"What about the Residence Act?" Madison asked. "Are you still hell bent on keeping the nation's capitol here in New York?"

"That's one of the reasons I've asked Senator Morris to join us. His financial acumen far surpasses mine and he and Pennsylvania have a lot at stake on the issue of assumption. Robert, you tell them," Hamilton said, waving his hand generously at his older friend.

"If you'll help pass Alexander's financial package, I'll change my vote and support the selection of the land along the Potomac River between Virginia and Maryland as our new capitol. My vote will break the deadlock and give that location the one vote margin it needs to settle the matter."

"That's it?" Jefferson asked. "I'm waiting for the other shoe to drop, Robert. You want something else, I'm sure of it. We've known one another too long."

"You are an untrusting soul, Thomas," Morris smiled, feeling a little like a boy having been caught with his hand in the cookie jar. "But you are quite right. I want Philadelphia to be the national capitol until the site adjoining Virginia is built. I understand it will take ten years so my 'City of Brotherly Love' will be our home for the next decade. Not an unreasonable request, is it?"

"You are true to your reputation, Robert. I'm sure you will have arranged a way to make a great deal of money from your largesse," Jefferson laughed. "And you, Hamilton, do you intend the national bank you want chartered to be located in Philadelphia as well?"

"Yes, the bank needs to be where the capitol is located."

"But you are seeking a twenty-year charter for the bank and Robert says it will only take half that time to build the new capitol. Why the discrepancy?"

"Easy," Hamilton said, his face turning crimson, "Because my friend Robert, here, and his friends, have insisted on it."

"I don't think Congress even has the authority to establish such a bank," Madison said, standing to his full 5'5" height. "I intend to make that case when Congress considers your proposal."

"You may do so and I will accept their judgment but, in the meantime, do we have an agreement?"

As Christmas 1790 approached, Robert Morris changed his vote and the Residency Act passed by a single vote. The process of constructing what would become the nation's capitol, Washington, District of Columbia, could now begin. It would not near completion until 1800 and, then President Thomas Jefferson would be its first executive occupant. Southern states, after meeting with Jefferson and Madison, agreed to support Alexander Hamilton's Assumption Act.

*****

The next few years didn't turn out as either Morris or Hamilton hoped, however.

"For God's sake, Alexander, what has your program gotten us into?" President Washington asked, unhappy with having agreed to his Treasury Secretary's proposal for a levy on whiskey.

"Every time General Neville, my tax collector, rides into western Pennsylvania, he's greeted by armed Americans threatening to blow his head off if he tries to collect the damn tax. Some of them even found out where he lived and they burned his house down. His wife and children were forced to move in with relatives. The newspapers are trumpeting this 'Whiskey Rebellion' as proof that the new Federal government has gone too far. We can't have Americans taking arms against their own government."

"Give it time, Mr. President," Hamilton said contritely. He hadn't expected this kind of reaction either. He could only hope it would simmer down. "We need that revenue, sir, and any other tax could be even more unpopular."

"Let's hope it does quiet down. I'm getting far too old and cranky to lead another war."

But the rebellion continued. Two years later, President Washington was forced to gather a militia force of 15,000 men to march against the rebels and suppress the insurgency. The Whiskey tax never raised as much money as Hamilton had predicted and the entire episode weakened the Federalist party and strengthened support for Thomas Jefferson and his Republicans.

Robert Morris was not idle during this period either. He turned his attention to making heavy land purchases surrounding the new capital whose location he had just supported. He purchased over six million acres on both sides of the Potomac River. He had made the commitment based on an expected loan from Holland's royal family but that loan never materialized because England and the Dutch declared war on France, where the Bourbon monarchy had been overthrown following the storming of the Bastille. The financial Panic of 1797 further unsettled European and American investments. The Napoleonic Wars that followed fifteen years later ruined the market for American lands and Morris's highly leveraged financial pyramid collapsed. At that time Robert Morris owned more land than any other American, but he didn't have enough *hard* money to pay his creditors. He was land poor, financially destitute, and he spent the final years of his life in debtor's prison.

II

THE FIRST CONSTITUTIONAL CRISIS

"The Electoral vote to determine the winner in the Presidential election of 1800 is as follows," the head of the Electoral Committee shouted in a stentorian voice. "73 votes for Thomas Jefferson of Virginia, 73 votes for Aaron Burr of New York, 65 votes for John Adams of Massachusetts, and 64 votes for Thomas Pinckney of South Carolina. We have the same number of electoral votes for Mr. Jefferson and Mr. Burr. We have a tie."

Thomas Jefferson

Aaron Burr

Shouts and fist thumping drowned out any attempt for him to continue. He banged his gavel again and again until the handle broke. It took another ten minutes for the room to settle down and those assembled to take their seats.

Outside, snow whirled through Philadelphia's narrow streets. It was mid-February 1801, and men from sixteen states had traveled long distances to be here. Kentucky, the newest state, had sent its two electors nearly seven hundred miles on horseback through terrible storms and near zero temperatures. One of South Carolina's representatives was absent due to illness and Georgia would be unable to cast one of its votes as a result of the sudden death of one of their electors. The rest of the men had arrived, short tempered and tired, to participate in what was becoming the first partisan election of their young country.

"Gentlemen, gentlemen, please!" he pleaded, hoping the electors were too exhausted to continue to vent their anger. "The Constitution is quite clear on this matter. You have voted; we have a tie. Whatever your intent, our task is over! We have fulfilled our responsibility. The matter will now be resolved by the outgoing House of Representatives. Either Mr. Jefferson or Mr. Burr will be our next President. This meeting is adjourned."

John Adams   **Gen Thomas Pinckney**

No one who had contributed to the writing of the Constitution had anticipated such a conundrum. The nation was barely a decade old and while it wasn't uncommon for some new unforeseen situation to arise, there had never been any issues of this magnitude.

The framers of the Constitution had established a system for electing a new President every four years. Voters in each state, white males...typically only those who owned property, would cast their votes, not for a candidate, but for 'Electors,' men who had indicated their preference for one candidate or another. It was understood that these men would generally follow the will of the voters in their respective states who had selected them, but it wasn't always obligatory for them to do so. These Electors would then travel to a common location to cast their vote. The candidate receiving the most votes would be declared the winner. None of this was necessary in America's first election. George Washington had received almost all of the 40,000 votes cast in 1788. John Adams had been chosen as his Vice-President. It was appropriate that someone from Virginia, the largest and most influential colony, and home of the man who had led the colonies through a frustrating, and underfunded, battle with the British, would hold the Presidency. It was equally appropriate that Massachusetts, the most vocal proponent of independence for the colonies, and its most obstreperous proponent, John Adams, would hold the Vice-Presidency.

Four years later, the election of 1792 reaffirmed the nation's earlier decision. It was no time to change leadership. Many people felt we should just make General Washington our monarch. It certainly has worked well for England, they thought. But George Washington had grown tired of the bickering. He had succeeded against overwhelming odds to oust the British. The Continental Congress, meanwhile, argued, rural states against more industrial ones, southern plantation owners against northern factory and business owners. Against whom would taxes be levied to pay for the war? Once money was raised, who would be paid first? There were still many citizens, many wealthy and influential, who felt the break from England, had been precipitous. They would have been happy to make their new nation a smaller version of what they'd known all their life…allegiance to a monarch. Now the aging General wanted nothing more than to sit and stare at the rolling hills of his plantation. He was eager to retire and return to his wife, Martha, and their estate at Mount Vernon.

Philosophical schisms, however, were becoming chasms and could easily tear the infant country apart before it reached puberty. One faction, led by Alexander Hamilton, and supported by the financiers of New York and Philadelphia, had been George Washington's selection as his Secretary of the Treasury. They favored a strong central government. Hamilton had aggressively been trying to convince the new President to establish a national bank similar to the one that controlled England's vast mercantile empire.

"Mr. President, I strongly urge you to reject Mr. Hamilton's proposal for a central bank," Thomas Jefferson urged, standing to every inch of his height.

"Sit down, Tom," Washington said, taking a deep breath, exhausted by the acrimony of his two most important cabinet members. "Alex, tone down your rhetoric and explain in terms a simple farmer like me can understand why we need such a bank."

"I'll try. It's quite simple. Right now we have thirteen separate states handling their own banking. Some have even issued their own currency. We'll never be able to deal in international markets unless our young nation has its own bank to control the country's money supply. This new bank, The First Bank of the United States, will be a clearing house for collecting revenues and paying government expenses. It will be privately owned, licensed by the Federal government to mint and issue money, and help the Federal government assume debts the states had incurred in fighting the war"

"And since it is to be private, its investors will reap huge profits. It is another of Mr. Hamilton's schemes to have the Federal government to usurp the power of the states."

Thomas Jefferson, Washington's Secretary of State, inventor, and founder of the University of Virginia, favored retention of the rural nature of the country and state's rights. Tall, urbane, and a romantic, he and Hamilton seemed to clash on every phase on how the young malleable United States should evolve. He imagined the country as a confederation of states with each man equal to his neighbor. He felt deeply about the philosophies he had espoused in his Declaration of Independence. Like-minded supporters, such as James Madison, founded the Democratic Republican party. They imagined the United States as a rural Eden, where the rights of the states were paramount to those of a Federal government.

"Thomas, I wanted you to know I intend to side with Hamilton on this issue of establishing a Federal bank," Washington said. It was a quiet evening and the street lights of Philadelphia were just being lit. One could still hear the hoofs of horses on the city's cobblestone streets. A servant had poured both men a glass of port and left them alone.

"It isn't a good decision, George." Only when they were alone did Jefferson deign to call the President by his Christian name.

"We aren't raising enough money to fund the government and pay our debts. The states continually bicker. I know you question Alex's motives but I fear we will continue to have thirteen points of view on this issue. We must move forward. And, I must tell you, I am exhausted. I seem to be spending more time refereeing you two, than providing leadership."

As the election of 1796 approached, these factions evolved into political parties, the Federalists and the Republicans. Their differences deepened and became more contentious. Newspapers in each city shouted and wrote scathing editorials favoring one view or the other. Who would replace General Washington? Attempts to convince him to remain as President for another four years had met with no success. He was tired. His long service to his country needed to end.

The Federalists nominated John Adams, Vice President under George Washington. The Republicans nominated Thomas Jefferson. Both men were respected national figures. They had championed independence from England. Adams had been Massachusetts's loudest voice in the Continental Congress. Jefferson was the young country's first Secretary of State. He had recently returned from France where he'd been successful in improving relations between the two countries.

Adams and the Federalists selected Thomas Pinckney, a Senator from South Carolina, to run as his Vice President. Pinckney had been successful in negotiating a treaty with Spain after the war and was admired by a wide swath of those who would vote. Adams understood he would need support from voters in the southern states if his party was to win the election.

Alexander Hamilton had been forced to the political sidelines by increasingly embarrassing rumors that he was having a prolonged affair...a dalliance, with a married woman, Maria Lewis Reynolds. Hamilton had been paying Mr. Reynolds, her husband, for more than three years to keep the relationship a secret but when personal letters between them were made public and printed, the handsome Scot had no alternative but to exit national politics. Jefferson was happy to see him go.

*****

"I'm going to run for President, Mr. Burr, and we are trying to select an appropriate candidate for Vice-President to campaign with me on the Republican ticket," Thomas Jefferson said. He had returned to the urban filth of Philadelphia from the comfort and gentleness of his beloved Monticello. A prematurely early snow already dusted the streets. Halloween was still weeks away. Within days rain was due and mix with horse dung and garbage. He preferred the respite of his plantation. His wife had died and he was lonely until he met Sally. She provided him the comfort and release a man needed. It invigorated him and allowed him to return to his responsibilities and hopes of evolving the Utopian society he envisioned.

He was sitting in a quiet alcove away from where the Congress had met most of the day. James Madison stood at his side, as Aaron Burr sat across from them. Burr was a large man and his confident demeanor made him appear even larger. His prominent aquiline nose brought images of Julius Caesar to mind, a connection Burr found most appropriate.

"I think I'd be an excellent choice, Mr. Jefferson. Your philosophies of government sit well with Virginia and the southern states but they are a little suspect in New York and Massachusetts. My stature in the north will give your party wider appeal. I believe the mantle of the Vice-Presidency would benefit you and suit me quite well."

"And your questionable reputation, Mr. Burr, how would we benefit from that?" Madison said, softly, wanting to measure the prickliness of the man.

"Why, Mr. Madison, you do speak. I always thought your words came from Mr. Jefferson, as a ventriloquist might, but I didn't even see him move his lips," Burr laughed.

"Do you deny that, while you have demonstrated your talents as an attorney these past years, your military reputation remains controversial?" Madison said, ignoring the insult.

"I had a brave and distinguished military career, Mr. Madison. I believe it was considerably more successful than yours." Burr's face turned crimson before he took a deep breath and turned his attention back to Jefferson.

"Are you asking me to join you in your quest for the Presidency because of John Adams or despite him? I admit I do not relish him becoming President, nor do I have any admiration for the Federalist hacks with which he surrounds himself. I do, however, possess considerable support among many wealthy individuals in the northern states."

"We just want to be sure you can withstand the rigors and insults that go with any campaign," Jefferson said, trying to return civility and calm to the room. "General Washington turned down your application to be a Brigadier General, did he not? He wrote, for all to see, *"By all that I have known and heard, Colonel Burr is a brave and able officer, but the question is whether he has not equal talents at intrigue."*

In a significant military engagement, Aaron Burr and a small regiment had saved Alexander Hamilton's Brigade from capture. He awaited a Commendation from General Washington for his actions. That recognition would mean a promotion and a significant rise in his stature. It never came and the relationship with the General he hoped for, never materialized. Washington's slight cast a permanent shadow on Burr's ambition and he left the military, turning his attention to a law career and New York politics.

The election of 1796 was hotly contested. It was the first time the nation had been asked to decide who its leaders would be. The selection of George Washington had been an easy one. No one else had his stature. This time, however, both men espoused different philosophies. The popular vote results weren't known for several weeks. John Adams had received 35,000 votes; Thomas Jefferson 31,000.

When the Electors met and the votes were counted, John Adams had received 71 electoral votes and was declared President. But no distinction of 'running-mate' existed, and Thomas Jefferson received 68 votes...more than Thomas Pinckney, and became Vice-President. The two highest officials in the country for the next four years would not be from the same political party nor share the same beliefs on how to govern.

The Constitution's Article II, Section 1, Clause 2 explained how Electors were to be selected:

> *Each State shall appoint, in such Manner as the Legislature thereof may direct, a Number of Electors, equal to the whole Number of Senators and Representatives to which the State may be entitled in the Congress: but no Senator or Representative, or Person holding an Office of Trust or Profit under the United States, shall be appointed an Elector.*

Clause 3 clarified the voting procedure for Electors:

> *The Electors shall meet in their respective States, and vote by Ballot for two Persons, of whom one at least shall not be an Inhabitant of the same State with themselves. And they shall make a List of all the Persons voted for, and of the Number of Votes for each; which List they shall sign and certify, and transmit sealed to the Seat of the Government of the United States, directed to the President of the Senate. The President of the Senate shall, in the Presence of the Senate and House of Representatives, open all the Certificates, and the Votes shall then be counted. The Person having the greatest Number of Votes shall be the President, if such Number be a Majority of the whole Number of Electors appointed; and if there be more than one who have such Majority, and have an equal Number of Votes, then the House of Representatives shall immediately choose by Ballot one of them for President; and if no Person have a Majority, then from the five highest on the List the*

said House shall in like Manner choose the President. But in choosing the President, the Votes shall be taken by States, the Representation from each State having one Vote; A quorum for this Purpose shall consist of a Member or Members from two thirds of the States, and a Majority of all the States shall be necessary to a Choice. In every Case, after the Choice of the President, the Person having the greatest Number of Votes of the Electors shall be the Vice President. But if there should remain two or more who have equal Votes, the Senate shall choose from them by Ballot the Vice President.

"When we were writing the Constitution, this was never the intent and you know it," John Adams said his face red. As soon as he'd heard the outcome of the electoral voting, he'd trudged through the snow and burst into Thomas Jefferson's office, where the tall, red-haired Virginian was having a meeting with James Madison and two other men.

"I'm afraid we have an urgent interruption, gentlemen, from a portly man who seems quite upset," Jefferson declared, as he stood, smiling. "Please excuse us. We can reconvene later. John," he said, his eyes twinkling as he turned his attention to his out of breath guest. Adams was busy removing his coat and scarf, clearly in a surly mood. "How nice of you to visit."

"If you were a gentleman, Jefferson, you'd resign and allow Pinckney to be sworn in as my Vice President."

"Then I guess I'm not a gentleman, John, because I certainly don't intend to resign and allow you and Hamilton's people to move our country toward becoming a Federal monarchy."

"Don't lump me in with that ambitious, devious, son of a bitch. You and I may not agree on many things, Thomas, but I have always trusted you. Hamilton, on the other hand, is nothing but slime. He has called me a poor imitation of Washington and too unstable to be President. He's been conniving with all the Electors in the northern states to vote for me and Pinckney to keep you from winning. Then he makes a special arrangement with Edward Rutledge in South Carolina to cast their votes for you and Pinckney. If he succeeded, Pinckney would have more votes than either of us and be the next President. I'm not sure which of us Hamilton dislikes the most."

"In that I defer to you, John. It was clever of him, you must admit. Pinckney would have been indebted to him and Hamilton would have returned to a position of influence and survived the stench of that long, sordid relationship with his paramour."

"It's well-known that he and I even disagree on which oysters are the most palatable. I, of course, favor those from the Chesapeake," Jefferson laughed, smiling at the short, stout man in front of him who could be most disagreeable. They had fought so many battles together through the years arguing for independence. And, although he often riled those around him, it was hard not to respect the intensity of his opinions.

"Jefferson, you are a rogue...charming, but a rogue. Keep your hunting dog, Madison, in line, at least. You and I will serve together, and may God save us all."

The following month Adams and Jefferson were sworn in as President and Vice President of the United States, each from a different political persuasion, each with a different agenda.

It was an unsettled period. The fledgling country had begun moving west into Kentucky and Tennessee. The charisma of George Washington as President and father of the country was gone and states floundered, trying to find their place vis a vis a central government. Adams and Jefferson found themselves at odds on almost every issue.

"You're making a mistake, John, appointing our mutual nemesis, Alexander Hamilton, to be head of the Army."

"Our esteemed Mr. Washington still holds that title but since he prefers retirement at Mount Vernon, we needed a strong spokesman, and Hamilton seems to have resurrected his reputation."

"You are naïve, Mr. Adams," Jefferson said, smiling as he began to exit the President's office. "He will wield his authority in ways best suited to him. I have already heard his various mantras, 'Conquer everything controlled by Spain that borders our country.' 'Be wary of an invasion from France.' 'Establish a tax to fund the likelihood of a war.' He is a fear monger eager to build whatever dominion he asserts as his. His demands to the new Congress are unending. You will rue your decision." Jefferson closed the door behind him.

Within months, John Adams began to realize that many members of his Cabinet, held over from Washington's Presidency, were yielding to Hamilton's influence.

Adams didn't hesitate to summarily fire them.

"There is certainly a hornet's test whirling around us, Thomas." James Madison was sprawled on the couch, his shoes off, a glass of port on the table nearby. It was the end of another contentious day. "Our friend, Aaron Burr, is obviously still upset at having lost his election as Vice-President. Now Hamilton is having at him."

"I know. Those two men had been close friends until Aaron chose to run for the Senate in New York and ended up defeating Alexander's father-in-law, General Patrick Schuyler. Alex turned on him. That man never forgets a slight. He's used his new position in the military to pressure our dear President to deny Burr a substantial military promotion and assignment."

"Of the two men, I don't care much for either one of them," Madison noted, downing his drink and rising to refill his glass.

"I don't think you care much for our President either," Jefferson noted, smiling at his friend's sarcasm.

"Look at what a mess he's making of this damn French affair. X,Y,Z…who thought up that silly reference for a

naval war between us and the Gauls."

"I know how sensitive those Frenchmen can be. I spent enough time in Paris," Jefferson said, stretching his long frame and rubbing the back of his neck. "Something Adams said offended them and they demanded an apology and money to expand trade between us. That trade is important."

"Of course," Madison laughed. "What would you do without your constant replenishment of French wine?"

"I do like a good bottle of their reds from Bordeaux. But, as I am led to believe, the hand of Alexander Hamilton has risen again. He's rumored to have taken huge bribes from the French to push the matter with Adams, and, at the same time, France was in a state of constant turmoil. Their constant European wars and their profligate monarchy that prefers to spend lavishly on themselves when their people are starving led them to revolution. James, it is axiomatic. Where money is to be found, you'll find our friend Hamilton."

A decade earlier, in the summer of 1789, events in France, four thousand miles, had shaken the confidence

of a young American government that had always considered the stability of France important to its well-being. A Parisian mob had stormed the famed Bastille, a large prison where French rebels, demanding democracy, were held, pending their execution on the guillotine. The angry throng then paraded through the streets, showing off the guards and soldiers they'd taken as captives, and crudely cutting off many heads. The National Guard tried to stop the crowds from looting, but it was useless. The mobs continued marching toward the palace. Upon learning that the Bastille had been taken, King Louis XVI, who was residing at Versailles, was reported to have asked one of his ministers: "Is this a revolt?" The minister, La Roche Foucault-Liancourt, replied, "No, Sire, it is a revolution." Little did Louis know that the mob's next goal was to march to Versailles, and take him away with them as well.

*****

"John, I plead with you," Jefferson said, hoping he held some sway with the President. "These Alien and Sedition Acts you are pushing to enact are a direct threat to the Bill of Rights you and I both fought to include in the Constitution."

"Thomas, with all due respect, France is in a state of upheaval and the possibility of revolt in this country cannot be overlooked. We must not permit radicals to foment another revolution. I will not have a crazy person gather with others in the public square demanding the overthrow of our government. I will not! If you and your Republican cohorts won't recognize the danger, we have enough

Federalist votes to enact these laws. We are not trying to silence opposition but we will suppress revolution."

"And how will you know the difference?" Jefferson said quietly, his shoulders bent as he walked dejectedly from the room.

Differences in the philosophies of Adams and Jefferson that had been a chasm had now become a canyon. A complete rupture of civility followed.

Steven Mason, the Senator from Virginia, stood at the dais, his hands shaking.

"My Federalist friends, I plead with you to reconsider what you are about to do. You are authorizing the President to deport any 'alien dangerous to the peace and safety of the United States' without defining what constitutes danger. You want to extend the time for an alien to become a citizen from two years to five. You are asking us to pass laws which will allow the President to deport any alien from a country at war with the United States, with particular emphasis on French citizens.

"We are a country that was established by those seeking escape from persecution…our parents and their friends. We are attempting to create a new land…one which tolerates free speech and is not afraid of it. If you pass these laws, we will be no better than the European monarchies from which our families fled."

His voice was drowned by shouts from the Federalist majority and the laws passed easily. John Adam's intent was clear. In a country where so many new people were flooding in seeking freedom from foreign countries, the American government would tolerate no dissent.

*****

"Thomas," James Madison shouted, bursting into his friend's office. "They've arrested Benjamin Bache...Ben Franklin's grandson. They've used the new Sedition Act to shut down his newspaper, *The Aurora*. They allege that he engaged in 'false, scandalous, and malicious writing' against the government and government officials. He's done no more than support our Republican principles."

"I'm sure he won't be the last. Damned Federalists have these new laws as a weapon to suppress all opposition and that includes everyone in our party. You'll see...this plague will spread. I thought this was all put to rest a half century ago when John Peter Zenger was acquitted of libel against the government. What did they say Bache did?"

"Apparently he has his grandfather's penchant for sarcasm and wit. He took editorial swipes at federal officials as being incompetent and involved in financial improprieties. But he saved his most acerbic writing for our President. He printed that Mr. Adams is 'blind, bald, crippled, toothless, and querulous, filled with nepotism and monarchial ambitions.' Officials wasted no time in arresting young Mr. Bache was arrested for libel under the new law."

Calling the Adams administration a 'continual tempest of malignant passions' and the President 'a repulsive pedant, a gross hypocrite, and an unprincipled oppressor,' James Callender published an unfavorable book and was sent to prison. When a cannon was fired to honor the President at a celebration in Newark, New Jersey, a man was overheard to say, 'There goes the President and they are firing at his ass.' Another man remarked that he didn't care 'if they fired through his ass.' That man was hauled off to jail, convicted of making seditious remarks, and fined. Much of the final two years of Adams admin-istration was thus spent, trying to shred the fabric of Republican muckraking. It didn't work. Instead, it unified the Republicans and gave them fodder for their claims that the Federalists had lost faith in democracy.

There was no question of who the principal combatants for the Presidency would be in 1800. John Adams and Thomas Jefferson would represent their parties. Thomas Pinckney and Aaron Burr would, once again, be their Vice-Presidential nominees. The divisiveness of the Federalist and Republican philosophies would be tested once more.

"I see that our old friend, Alexander Hamilton, has regained enough power to become an influential 'shadow' presence in New York," Madison said, as he and his friend, Jefferson, and several aides, poured over the most recent information on the political situation around the country.

"Not surprising," Jefferson responded. "He and Aaron Burr will knock heads often, trying to seek the votes of New

Yorkers. It isn't an easy state to control. The farmers upstate differ greatly from their brethren in the city."

"The Federalists will continue to dominate New England with their message of a strong central government and pro-British leanings," Madison said. "We continue to do well among the southern states with their desire for a decentralized government and pro-French stance. A most popular position since the overthrow of King Louis and the Bourbon monarchy. They're quite angry about the tax President Adams levied to pay for his undeclared war against the French... It is most unpopular. The Alien and Sedition acts and their aggressive prosecutions frightened many who had not made up their mind. Our people continue to speak loudly that such laws are a danger to our Bill of Rights."

In the end Thomas Jefferson and his Republican-Democrats received 41,000 votes. John Adams and his Federalists received 26,000 votes. Jefferson also received the majority of electoral votes. He would be the new President, or so it was assumed.

Both the Federalists and the Republicans were well aware of the electoral debacle that had arisen four years earlier and had propelled Jefferson into the Vice-Presidency that was intended for Thomas Pinckney. Neither party wanted to make that mistake again. One of the Federalist electors was to vote for John Jay instead of Pinckney, giving Adams a one vote margin. The Republicans had planned to do something similar. But lost somewhere in each party's election enthusiasm the plan failed. The events of 1796 were about to repeat themselves.

"I can't believe we let the same thing happen...again," John Adams thundered. "At least it will be the outgoing House of Representatives where we have a majority who resolves this idiocy."

"John, who are you shouting at?" Abigail Adams said, walking in from the adjoining room.

"The incompetence of politicians. One of our electors was to keep our Presidential and Vice-Presidential votes from being the same as it was in the last election but someone messed up and now the election decision will need to be decided by Congress. At least it's the house dominated by we Federalists. The batch of new Republicans that were elected had not yet been sworn into office and the Congressional Federalists who were leaving office would never vote for Jefferson, a Francophile they detested...anyone but Jefferson!"

As John Adams predicted the outgoing Federalist congressmen voted for Aaron Burr, denying election to Thomas Jefferson. For seven days in early February, every tally ended up the same...73 votes for Jefferson, 73 for Burr. States voted as a unit and it would take a majority, nine of the sixteen to settle the issue. Again, the result was 8-7, no majority. Vermont was split evenly and cast a blank ballot. The Federalists would not waver in their resolve to keep Jefferson from the Presidency. The Representatives were frustrated and becoming increasingly antagonistic toward one another.

*****

The House retired for a long weekend. James Bayard, the Congressman from Delaware, was eager to return to his family in Wilmington. He slept much of the carriage ride home that Friday. It was a harsh, uncomfortable ride and he kept being jerked awake as the horses sought purchase on the soggy and iced over, pot-holed road. It was near midnight when he arrived. He kissed his wife, pulled off his boots, and fell into a deep sleep until late the following morning.

James Bayard

"You have a visitor, James," his wife, Nancy said, pulling aside the drapes to let the grey winter light into the room. "I hope you haven't brought business home, the children have missed you."

"Who is it?"

"I'm told it's Mr. Hamilton, although why he should come to our home on a weekend, and uninvited, I don't know. It is quite inappropriate."

"That's Hamilton. Social grace was never his strong feature," Bayard smiled. "Offer him some tea and show him to my office. I'll be down in several minutes. Then get the children ready for the day. We'll play some games inside since it's far too cold to go the beach."

James Bayard's family was descended from Peter Stuyvesant, one of New York's founders, when it was a Dutch colony called New Amsterdam. Nancy's father, Richard Bassett, was a member of the Constitutional Convention. Both were confirmed Delaware Federalists.

"Mr. Hamilton, how nice of you to visit, albeit unexpectedly," James Bayard said, attempting only slightly to mask his irritation.

"I apologize, James, but the exigencies of the situation demand it. Will you continue to vote with your colleagues for John Adams?" he asked.

"Alex," he said, using the shortened version of Hamilton's name, an appellation he knew the man disliked. "How I vote is my decision and in concert with other Representatives from Delaware. I don't appreciate your asking, especially in light of current rumors that have been circulating."

"Rumors? What rumors?"

"Is it true you've been trying to get all of the southern Electors to switch from Adams to Pinckney?"

"I've discussed it with a few friends," Hamilton admitted. "I believe we've had about all of John Adams the country can stomach. I will do anything to assist in returning to his wife, Abigail, in Massachusetts."

"Well, Hamilton," Bayard said, shaking his head. "You are a chameleon, no doubt about it. You turn faster than a wind vane. You've always been a Federalist. Adams let you run the Army and now you abandon both. You'd rather have Jefferson and his Republicans, that's what you're saying."

"That's not what I'm saying. The Federalists lost this election. What I'm saying is that we have to recognize it. Aaron Burr would make a terrible President. We need to stop making a charade of the process. I want you to think long and hard on our options. I don't like Madison and his minions but Jefferson is more pragmatic. I want you to speak to him before you make your decision. I'll leave you now to your family. Please apologize to Mrs. Bayard for my intrusion. I know she comes from a political family, however, so she may be slightly empathetic."

Bayard's weekend was shorter than he intended. He and his six children did manage a game of croquet on the back lawn in the brief afternoon sun.

"Not easy to swing a mallet when you're wearing a coat," James complained, good-naturedly. "All four of the boys beat me and I think I only beat our two daughters because you've taught them to be tactful."

Nancy laughed. It was a special occasion when the entire family sat down and enjoyed dinner together. It had been nearly a month and she knew the children relished putting on nice clothes and being treated like adults. They dined on roast pork, potatoes and minced apples. The two older boys were allowed a small glass of wine and James Bayard watched, swelling inside at his good fortune. We must have good leadership for the next four years, he thought, for Nancy, for the children, and for the entire country.

Sunday the weather turned temperate. He and his wife enjoyed a quiet and loving evening together, nestled under a heavy goose comforter. Now, having enjoyed his children and breakfast, he prepared to return to Philadelphia.

"This warmth is going to make the roads muddy, you know," Nancy said as her husband prepared to leave.

"I know, but I have no choice. Hamilton has arranged for me to have a private dinner with Jefferson…very hush-hush."

"Well, don't let that slick, handsome man, bedevil you."

"Handsome? So you think he's handsome. Seems it is you he has bedeviled."

"Is it true he has several mistresses, including some of color at Monticello?"

"I don't know. Would you like me to ask him?" Bayard laughed.

"Of course not," she said, suddenly rethinking the possibility. "He wouldn't tell you, would he?"

"Nancy, we aren't meeting to discuss his sex life. Kiss the children for me."

*****

"Mr. Jefferson," James Bayard said as he entered a small private dining room in the back of a popular tavern.

"Mr. Bayard," Jefferson said, standing to shake hands, his head inches from the rafters overhead. "Thank you for agreeing to meet with me. I apologize for taking you away from your family."

The two men had known one another through the years but their differing approach to the role government should play had kept any meaningful friendship from developing. "Hamilton said you wanted to meet and, frankly, it came as quite a surprise, especially from that man."

"If it's alright, I'd prefer to chat after dinner. They have a wonderful wine cellar here and I've taken the liberty of ordering two different French Bordeaux's. They're from 1792, a very good year. Are you a fan of good wine, Mr. Bayard? I have a large cellar at Monticello and I'd be happy to arrange a case to be sent to you in Wilmington."

"Thank you, but no. We're moderate drinkers and have neither your wine education, nor your cultured palette."

Two hours later, dinner was over, and the plates had been removed. Fresh candles had been set in place and the room was brighter, as much from the two bottles of wine, as from the candles.

"Excellent meal, Mr. Jefferson. Now we should get to our business. I spent a long day in the carriage getting here and my eyes will grow heavy all too soon."

"Of course, James. It is simple. I need you to break ranks and vote for me. Your single vote will break the stalemate and we can move on to governing."

"Is that all? And I thought this would be complicated. Seriously, Mr. Jefferson, why would I do that?"

"Hamilton feels certain that a prime concern of yours is what happens to all the Federalist

Appointees that Adams has put in place. Is that true?"

"It's certainly one concern. Most of them are doing a fine job and I think it is disruptive to the government if every new President dispatches people who have performed."

"I agree," Jefferson said quietly.

"You do?"

"I do," Jefferson said, smiling.

"You realize this doesn't mean I intend to become a Republican or to support your policies. I believe them to be misguided, and I will do all I can to block them."

"Fair enough."

*****

In a separate dining room on the outskirts of Philadelphia Alexander Hamilton was continuing his efforts to deny the Presidency to Aaron Burr as he met with a group of Representatives from Massachusetts.

"I want you to switch your votes to Jefferson. He is by far a less dangerous man than Burr. Trust me; I've worked with them both. At least Jefferson has integrity."

"A strange concept," one delegate voiced, "Alexander Hamilton lecturing us on integrity. Politics does make strange bedfellows." Hamilton overheard him and blanched, but said nothing.

*****

On the 36th ballot, on February 17, 1800, James Bayard changed his vote from Aaron Burr to blank. That was all that was needed to break the deadlock. Delaware now went into the Republican column, giving Thomas Jefferson the nine states he needed to reach a majority. A new President had been selected. Aaron Burr would be Vice-President but the relationship between he and the President had been ruptured beyond repair.

Nor would Aaron Burr forget Hamilton's role in his failure to win the Presidency. His dislike for the man festered like a prickle under his saddle. The week after the new President's inauguration Hamilton announced his intention to withdraw from the Federalist party he had helped establish if Burr became their presidential candidate in the next election.

In 1804 Alexander Hamilton helped defeat Aaron Burr's effort to become Governor of New York. Slurs were hurled by each side but Burr, believing his honor had been attacked, demanded an apology. Hamilton refused and Burr demanded a duel to settle the insult. On July 11th, on the west bank of the Hudson River, the men met at dawn. Only their seconds were present to witness Burr shoot his enemy with a single bullet that struck Hamilton in his lower abdomen. He died the following afternoon.

*****

The election of Thomas Jefferson was the first of a string of Republican Presidents. He purchased the Louisiana territory from France, doubling the size of the country. He dispatched Lewis and Clark to seek a northwest passage to the Pacific. The Alien and Sedition Acts were repealed and everyone convicted under those laws was released. James Bayard remained true to his word. His single vote had resolved the impasse. The Federalists had become a diminished voice, but of those, Bayard's remained the loudest.

III

CHANGING THE NATION'S FINANCIAL DIRECTION

"Mr. President, good of you to see me so late in the evening."

"Salmon, this office is always open to you," Abe Lincoln said, amicably to his Secretary of the Treasury, Salmon P. Chase. "Have you had your dinner yet? I'm sure the kitchen can put together a plate for you. Mrs. Lincoln and I were served a tasty lamb roast."

"No, no thank you."

Salmon Chase was the antithesis of this man before him. Lincoln was home spun...Chase was urbane, convinced he was destined to be President. Somehow fate had stepped in to reverse their roles. But Salmon Chase was certain the error would be remedied in the next election.

Salmon Chase's father had died when he was a young boy and along with ten siblings, his mother struggled to raise her family. But Salmon was a bright boy and remained in school, eventually graduating from Dartmouth

College and moving to Cincinnati in pursuit of a career in law. His first cases were defending fugitive slaves who had escaped from their masters on southern plantations.

56

Their suffering made him a staunch anti-slave advocate and helped him get elected Senator and later, Governor of Ohio.

Speaking before juries developed him into becoming an ardent orator. It also propelled him into being a prominent choice for the Republican nomination for President in 1860. His anti-slavery views made him a close friend of Harriet Beecher Stowe and his politics dated back to Martin Van Buren, thirty years earlier. He was one of the most well-known Republicans at the recent party Convention, leader of the faction called Radical Republicans and certainly its most articulate voice against slavery. But it was his vocal objection to high tariffs that upset influential eastern Republicans and, having such an outspoken position, made him unacceptable as an unyielding Presidential nominee. Instead the party, deeply divided, had settled on an unknown, a 'dark horse' from Illinois, Abraham Lincoln. Tall and gangly, Lincoln was more known for his iconic wit and debates with Stephen Douglas. Chase would likely try again in 1864 if the war was over. He was used to the bright lights of national politics and his appetite to be President had been whetted.

The newly elected President, Abraham Lincoln, surprised everyone by asking each of the men who were his rivals for the Republican nomination, all better known, to join him in running the country. Lincoln, a little Senator, and a 'hick' from rural Illinois, had been a dark horse candidate. He had been selected when those who would decide could not agree on an alternative. He had easily defeated two Democratic

Party candidates, divided over the question of slavery and secession.

Now in support of the new President, they all agreed to serve, surprised at the largesse of this man they had initially treated with disdain. Salmon P. Chase joined the cabinet as Secretary of Treasury to oversee the nation's financial affairs. William Seward, an outspoken opponent of slavery and a Senator from New York, accepted an appointment as Secretary of State. Edward Stanton, an ardent anti-secessionist and Attorney General under President Buchanan, agreed to become Secretary of War.

Salmon P. Chase   **A young Abraham Lincoln**

A war between the states had evolved into a tragic but foregone conclusion. This was 1861 and there would be long months and many lives lost before the issues that brought about the decision of the southern states to secede from the Union resolved themselves. The outcome would remain in doubt for some time. Lincoln had made it clear in a speech he'd given in 1858, *'a house divided against itself cannot stand.'*

Salmon Chase knocked on the door of the President's office, continuing to realize how someone should have been knocking on his door. He still anguished over his rejection as the Republican standard bearer. 'President Chase' had a ring to it. Maybe 1864 would be his opportunity.

"Come in. Salmon, how nice to see you," President Lincoln said, standing politely. He motioned his guest to the couch and spread his long frame.

"How are the plans for executing the war against Jefferson Davis and his henchmen proceeding?" Chase asked, getting comfortable at this stark, lanky man he still didn't fully understand.

"Slowly, far too slowly." The Confederates have moved their capitol to Richmond…much too close to Washington, and Robert E. Lee is making great strides getting their forces organized. You know, I'd offered him command of all Union forces, but he declined. His loyalty to his state of Virginia was unwavering, he said."

"Do you think General Winfield Scott is up to the task?" Chase asked, his forehead wrinkling at the realization that these would have been his decisions to make. "After all he's seventy-four years old and has the gout. And the last war he fought, against Mexico was fifteen years ago. I'm sure weapons or tactics must have changed since then."

"We can only hope. He's certainly our most senior general, but he doesn't possess the acumen of Robert E. Lee, of that I'm certain."

"I don't envy you, or Secretary of War Stanton, the task of prosecuting this war. It is so unfortunate that the southern states found it necessary to leave the Union. But I didn't come to commiserate with you, Mr. President. I came to discuss how we're going to pay for the war. We are going to need to raise a great deal of money."

"Our gold reserves aren't enough?" the President asked, his brow furrowing.

"Not nearly," Chase explained. "If you recall, we had a national bank until 1830 when its charter expired. That was the Second National Bank of the United States. Since then the states have pretty well done what they want. At the present time there are more than sixteen hundred charter banks spread throughout the country. It's pretty chaotic. The Federal government can borrow from these banks but I don't think we can raise enough money that way."

"What do you suggest?" Lincoln asked, grabbing a shawl from a chair and putting it over his shoulders. He walked to a nearby door and opened it.

"Luther, would you bring us some tea and some of Mrs. William's shortbread? Salmon, would you like something more substantial?" he said turning toward his guest.

"I think I'd prefer a brandy."

"There's a carafe on the sideboard, please help yourself. I'm beginning to suspect we'll be here awhile."

Salmon Chase took a hefty swallow and waited for the President to get comfortable before continuing.

"We need to get the Federal government back into the banking business by chartering Federal banks and allowing them to issue bank notes secured by U.S. government bonds. These banks would buy the bonds and provide a continuous market for us to finance the war."

"What makes you think the Congress will pass such an act?"

"I'm not sure what this Congress will pass but there will be many among them who will understand the urgency of our needing to procure the men and materiel necessary to prosecute this war."

"Go ahead, Salmon. If you can convince the Congress to pass such a bill, I'll sign it."

*****

"Chase, I'll fight you on this," Thaddeus Stevens said. The Secretary of the Treasury had come to Congressman Steven's office in the building that housed all the members of Congress. As a Representative from Pennsylvania, it wasn't a large office, but Stevens didn't care. He was far more effective as a radical Republican on the floor of the house than having spats with people from the Executive Branch in his office.

Stevens was witty, with a flamboyant and acerbic style that often left both his admirers and critics laughing. But he was not to be trifled with. He had a strong sense of the need for equality among all men. His energies had resulted in the passage of laws providing free education in Pennsylvania and, since the war had begun, he had grown more and more focused on the plight of fugitive slaves. But he understood finance as well.

"We need to finance the war, Thaddeus. This is a sound way to do it."

"You say 'sound.' I say that all it does is line the pockets of the bankers. Why can't the government issue the bonds directly to the public? The Government and not the banks should have the benefit from creating the medium of exchange."

"Thaddeus, the country doesn't possess enough gold reserves to pay for this war if it lasts beyond one year."

"Then we have a year to consider our options, don't we?" Stevens said stubbornly.

As 1861 came to an end money shortages were beginning to be felt in all the large eastern cities, such as New York, Boston, and Philadelphia. It would no longer be possible to exchange money for gold or silver as they had been obligated to do. Confederate successes on the battlefield were making it clear the war would not be a short term skirmish. The Union army was going to need significantly more men and artillery if they were to prevail...losing the war was an unacceptable option.

"Immediate action is of great importance. The treasury is nearly empty," Treasury Secretary Salmon P. Chase told Congress in February, 1862. "The country clearly has to revamp its policies or we will face financial ruin."

"Eventually you are all going to come around to my way of thinking," Elbridge Gerry Spaulding, one time Mayor of Buffalo, New York and now a congressman, said to a filled meeting of the House. He had foreseen the problem and had a solution ready.

"All our government needs to do is print money to pay for the Civil War and assure the public it's valid."

"That's economic heresy," another Congressman laughed. "What you propose is just print worthless paper...'fiat money'...money that is money not because it is backed by gold or silver, but because some nameless official in the government says it is money."

Thaddeus Stevens and the Radical Republican faction of the party weren't sure it would work either but they liked the idea of a financial system between the people and the government with no chance for bankers to intercede and take a hefty profit. They began referring to it as the *"greenback"* system, the issuance of paper currency, called 'greenbacks' because of their color. They would be fiat United States notes guaranteed by the Federal government.

Greenback Currency

A week after Chase's warning and his failure at getting a national bank established. Congress passed the first Legal Tender Act, which authorized the printing of $150 million in Treasury notes. The bills were printed on only one side with green ink. The name "greenbacks" stuck. They proved to be universally popular and remarkably sound. It was Chase's responsibility to design the notes. In an effort to further his political career, his face appeared on a variety of U.S. paper currency, starting with the $1 bill so that the people would recognize him. He admired Lincoln but he continued to chafe at failing to win the Republican nomination. The fire to be elected President in 1864 when the next presidential contest would take place continued to burn in his marrow.

*****

"Jay, I need your help," Chase said, pacing the carpeting in his office at the capital. He had invited Jay Cooke, a wealthy New York financier to Washington. Despite initial favorable reaction, it was going to be necessary to convince the public that these bonds were a good investment. It would take someone with the resources to make that case.

"You raised three million dollars for the State of Pennsylvania through your new bank in Philadelphia. Now I need you and your people to sell these new bonds the Federal government is issuing.

Cooke accepted the task with relish. His profits would be substantial. He hired agents to travel the country, touting the new bonds, "5/20's", callable in five years, due in twenty. They heralded a new type of patriotism based on liberal notions of self-interest. Editorials, handbills, and signs appealed to the desire of individual Americans to turn a profit, while simultaneously aiding the war effort. The initial financing of the Union's war effort was accomplished and Chase breathed a sigh of relief.

It was time for the Treasury Secretary to try once more to get Congressional approval for his National Bank to be established. Greenbacks were fine but they weren't enough to fund a protracted war. Once again Thaddeus Stevens and the Radical Republican faction of the party opposed it, angry at the exorbitant profits Cooke and his people had made. The Eastern banks and the influence they could purchase with their financial resources opposed establishment of the bank. They were quite happy with the state banking system. Each of their banks was a bigger fish in a smaller pond, able to influence the outcome of local and statewide elections. A national bank would destroy their power.

An angry Salmon Chase decided to use his leverage with the President.

"Mr. Lincoln, I have decided to resign if I don't get your full support establishing a government owned national bank."

"Salmon, you do understand the problems you would create by resigning, don't you?" A tired Lincoln sighed. It had been a bad day...the worst of a bad week. The war was not turning out to be a simple matter. "A substantial segment of our Republican party relies on your presence to guide the administration. We are in the midst of a war, for God's sake."

"And you have asked me to finance that war. Thaddeus Stevens and bankers around the country are thwarting that effort. You can exert pivotal influence. Instead, your silence is being viewed as less than enthusiastic support."

"If I support you, I antagonize them. I need us pulling together. We're now on our third General trying to run the Union Army. So far they've been a hapless group. They're more given to planning and parading than fighting...more to ass-sitting than engaging the Confederate Army. We've been out-Generaled and out-fought," Lincoln said with great frustration.

"Nevertheless, whoever you choose to lead our forces will need to pay the troops and purchase cannon. This is the best way to accomplish that goal. Support it or find someone else to finance this war," Chase threatened. Lincoln sat back in his old rocker. He closed his eyes and rocked silently for several minutes while silence hung heavily in the room. Chase was transfixed, wondering whether the President had fallen asleep. Finally Lincoln stood, his shoulders stooped, and nodded to his old adversary.

"I will give your efforts my full support," he said.

With the President now behind him, Chase proposed the National Currency Act of 1863. It would create the position of Comptroller of the Currency to monitor the nation's money supply and set long-term economic goals to finance the war and stabilize the availability of money. Along with Thaddeus Stevens and his Radical Republican cohorts, Hugh McCollough, President of the Bank of Indiana, lent his energies to defeating the bill.

"State banks can do the job," he proclaimed.

Lobbying for and against passage was fierce. The nine Democrats, those from the Border States, and four members of the Union party voted 'no' as a bloc. It would be up to the Republicans to resolve the matter and they were divided. Those from the West and the 'radical' wing opposed the bill. Those from the East and friends of Chase supported it. The vote was deadlocked.

The decision would rest with an unassuming Senator from Rhode Island, Henry Anthony, former editor of the Providence Journal and later, Governor of the tiny state. As a publisher he was virulently anti-Catholic, riling against the influx of Irish and French Catholics moving into his state. But he was also an abolitionist and supporter of the President. In the Senate, however, he preferred the role of conciliator. Being in the center of a storm was not comfortable for him.

Senator Henry Anthony

"Henry," Abe Lincoln said, greeting the heavy-set Senator, and welcoming him to the White House. Many of the President's supporters were not pleased with his energized efforts to support the new currency legislation and Henry Anthony was among them. "You know Secretary Chase, of course."

"Certainly, how are you, Salmon?"

"As frustrated, as we all are."

"These are difficult times," Lincoln said. "We took heavy losses at Fredericksburg. Lee moved his forces forward most effectively while our General McClellan sat with his rear-end...and his troops, firmly planted in cement. Secretary Stanton replaced him with General Burnside. Burnside was only good for parades. His lack of leadership in battle cost us hundreds of lives. Now Stanton has appointed General Hooker. Our troops are getting discouraged."

"We must have a General with balls somewhere in a blue uniform," Chase said, as the other two winced at the off-color remark.

"Ordering all the slaves in the south to be free was a clever move," Senator Anthony said, hoping to reset the tone in the room. "Do you think they'll revolt against their white masters?"

"Probably not, but the Rebels may have to divert some of their troops from the field, just in case. And, remember, I didn't free the slaves in the Border States like Kentucky, just the slaves from the nine states that seceded."

"Yes, I know. Thaddeus Stevens and his group would have preferred a complete abolition of slavery."

"I would have, as well," the President acknowledged, but it would have alienated states where we need support. As it is, our Generals are keeping all the runaway slaves they encounter and setting them free, even in the Border States."

"Your Emancipation Proclamation was a powerful statement, Mr. President," Chase said in sincere admiration.

"Thank you, but our Generals are demanding more troops. We're going to be submitting a bill for mandatory conscription. They tell me that we'll need another eight divisions if we're going to win this war," Lincoln said, exhaustion creeping into his voice.

"The Congress will support that," Anthony said, "But I'm not sure how popular it will be with the general public."

"Henry," Salmon Chase said, standing for emphasis, "We need you to support my National Banking bill that the Congress is considering and I need you to help persuade the other undecided Senators, such as Howard of Michigan and Howe from Wisconsin." The frustrated Treasury Secretary was not given to long periods of subtlety. He was anxious to get the issue resolved.

"That's why we've asked you here, Henry," the President said, embarrassed by the tactlessness with which

the issue had been set forth. It wasn't his style. "I've always appreciated the independence of your decisions but as Salmon said, we need your support. I'm not a fan of applying Presidential pressure but I've run out of alternatives."

"And I'm going to resign if I can't get this bill passed. I can find no other way to finance this war," Chase said.

"I don't really like the idea of a national bank and a national currency, Salmon," Senator Anthony replied. "It smacks of usurping the power of the states, more federalism, and more centralization of authority. If this continues why even have states at all?"

"The states aren't fighting this war," Chase said, raising his voice. "They are supporting a national effort to keep the Union together and we need to raise money at the Federal level to finance it."

"I can ask them to support it, but I can't do so with any enthusiasm," Anthony said, breathing deeply, unhappy with the task the President and Chase were asking him to perform.

"Henry, what would make this more palatable to those opposing the bill?" Lincoln asked, sharing afternoon tea with the influential Senator.

"What if you agree to make Hugh McCulloch Comptroller of the Currency?" Senator Anthony asked.

"McCulloch?" Chase said, stunned at the suggestion. "The man has been most vocal in his opposition. He owns a state bank that would suffer if the bill is passed."

"True, but he's bright and sensible. He's also influential enough to convince other state bankers and a few undecided Senators that the bill is necessary. Salmon Chase and the President looked at one another and nodded.

Hugh McCulloch

A week later, having secured McCulloch support, Senator Anthony changed his vote. The final vote for passage was now 23-21. The impasse had been broken by a single vote.State banks would now be taxed on notes they issued and these taxes slowly drove the banks from existence. The new federal currency, backed by the United States government, grew in acceptance, and the financing of the war was assured. Senator Anthony later became President Pro Tem of the body he endeared. His single vote had made the difference.

IV

THE IMPEACHMENT OF
ANDREW JOHNSON

"Oh, my God....the President has been shot!"

*****

It had only been a few months since President Lincoln met with the three men who had challenged him for the nomination four years earlier. They were now his Cabinet and closest advisors. Salmon Chase of the Treasury, Edward Stanton of the War Department, and William Seward, Secretary of State, sat quietly on the White House's back veranda. A nattily attired waiter walked among them silently, offering cold drinks and small canapés. The lanky, soft-spoken man with the deep-sunken eyes, watched, asking about their wives and children. They had each come to respect the man's genuine humanity. He had aged terribly in the past four years. Each new on his face seemed to represent the memory of another young Union soldier who had died in combat.

Once the waiter left, Lincoln turned to the topic at hand.

"I've decided to replace Hannibal Hamlin as Vice-President on the ticket. His views and speeches have become more and

"Can't you speak to him?" Chase asked. "Changing the ticket is most unusual."

"I agree and I've spoken to him on several occasions. I pleaded with him to tone down his rhetoric but he wants to wreak havoc and revenge on the south at a time when we're finally winning the war. We want our fathers and brothers in the southern states to believe they will be welcomed back into the Union. Hamlin's vitriol does the opposite. I am willing to consider any of you if you're interested in being on the ticket, but frankly, each of you is so critical to our struggle in your present positions, it is my hope you will remain there."

Each of them respectfully declined. Each had their own thoughts and designs on running for President in 1868 and they had far more authority and visibility in their Cabinet positions than they would have as a toothless Vice-President.

*****

Once the President had asked him, Andrew Johnson, to run as his Vice-President, a whirlwind of campaigning for

the upcoming 1864 election had been undertaken around the country. It was an appropriate selection. The message was simple...let's end this war and heal the nation. The quiet Senator from Tennessee, a border state, gave proof to the President's sincerity. It had all happened so quickly...less than a year ago, but Andrew Johnson's enthusiasm for sharing the Republican ticket with a man he admired would forever alter his life.

It had only been a month since the Republican ticket of Abraham Lincoln and Tennessee Senator Andrew Johnson won the election. With only the Northern states and those out West allowed to cast ballots, it was a mostly uncontested event. Only weeks later, a somber General Robert E. Lee surrendered to Ulysses S. Grant at the Appomattox Court House. Heavy Confederate losses had taken the last energies and hope that the South could continue to wage war. There were still units of the Confederate Army fighting and those pockets of resistance were taking needless Confederate and Union lives. The years of internecine bloodshed were nearly over.

The gangly, tired looking President, a shawl around his stooped shoulders, had acquiesced to his wife's request for a quiet evening out. There was a new play at the Ford theatre. It would allow him a few hours distraction. His controversial selection of the heavy drinking, cigar chomping, Ulysses S. Grant to run the Union Army had proven to be the right one. The man had met and beaten his adversary's best efforts. Abraham Lincoln had succeeded in holding the Union together. The House divided was no more.

Less than a mile away, Andrew Johnson and Eliza, his wife, were still unpacking and getting their five children settled in their new Washington D.C. home. Andrew Johnson, tailor, businessman, and Tennessean, had been the only Senator from a southern state to remain in the Senate when twenty-one of his Senatorial colleagues, all from Southern states, and a large number of Congressmen from

the Lower House stormed out following the rancorous
election of Lincoln in 1860. Within the month the sovereign
state of South Carolina had sent troops to capture the federal
facility at Fort Sumter that had guarded the entry to
Charleston harbor since the Revolutionary War. Shots were
fired by that state's militia in a blatant repudiation of the
Federal government.

The formation of the Confederate States of America was
no longer just a threat...it had become a reality All those years
and efforts trying to reach a compromise had come to naught.
It was war, war against those who had been friends and kin
days earlier. Brother against brother, partner against partner,
parents against children! The elders across the country could
still remember fighting the British forty years earlier. A few
even remembered, in awed nostalgia, doubling the size of
their small country when President Jefferson purchased the
Louisiana territory from the French. In the decades that
followed, however, unity and patriotism had given way to
economic divides, state's rights, and slavery. Four states,
South Carolina, Mississippi, Florida, and Texas, seceded from
the Union as soon as they understood the northern
Republican bloc they would face in Congress. With Abe
Lincoln in the White House they would be rendered mute
and ineffective. Alabama, Georgia, and Louisiana followed
quickly. Lincoln's call for more troops, following South
Carolina's attack on the Federal arsenal at Fort Sumter,
brought a swift response from four more states, Virginia,
Arkansas, Tennessee, and North Carolina. Divisiveness in

Virginia led to the formation of a new state, West Virginia. Kentucky, declaring neutrality, along with Missouri, formed 'rump' governments not fully recognized by the Federal government or the Confederacy. Nine states in all, some among the original thirteen colonies, had chosen to leave the United States and establish their own nation.

*****

"Eliza, put those dishes down. Please, come sit on the porch and talk to me. It's so pleasant in the evening this time of year here in Washington, a little nip in the air, spring around the corner."

President Andrew Johnson

"I hope we're happy here, Andrew. The children all think it's a grand adventure but I'd rather be home in Knoxville."

"Imagine us, here in the Capitol," Andrew Johnson said, exhaling a circle of smoke from his pipe. "Four years of war.

How many of our kin lie dead or missing a limb from grapeshot? How many crops never got planted?"

"More than I care to remember," Eliza said, sadly.

"I remember when Senator Nicholson asked me to join him in walking out of the Senate. 'The people of Tennessee deserve a unified voice, Andrew,' he said. 'We cannot brook Federal interference in our affairs.'

"'Then let's stay and change their minds,'" I said. "We've inherited our responsibilities from Andrew Jackson. He would never have agreed to divide our country. But he just looked at me, turned around, and took his tall dejected body out of the chamber, his head down, his arm around John Calhoun's shoulders. It was such a sad moment for me. He'd been such a friend and mentor for so many years. After that the Senate chamber seemed ghostly, echoes reverberating from the rafters, nearly half of its members gone. The session was cancelled for the remainder of the day.

"It's hard to believe that was four years ago. So much happened so quickly after that, so many people killed, and now, here we are, you and me, helping run the country. I confess I thought I'd always be nothing more than a tailor. Now Mr. Lincoln's confidence has vaulted me into being the Vice-President of these United States, with an opportunity to make a real difference. I don't want to disappoint him."

"Andrew," Eliza smiled, "You were never just a tailor."

"I was certainly illiterate. You had to teach me arithmetic and my readin' and writin' was pretty limited. I never understood how you found the time to be such a good teacher while taking care of our five children. I love you, you know."

"You've always made me proud of you. I remember when you tried to pass a law giving free farm land to the poor...that took a special kind of a man and explains why so many people always took to you."

"Eliza, I grew up dirt poor, never enough to eat. My father died when I was three. My mother took in washing and mending for rich families. It wasn't a childhood I remember fondly. I'd see those wealthy folks in their big carriages not caring about no one..."

"Anyone," Eliza corrected.

Suddenly the evening's quiet was shattered. Shouts from the street rang out and people began running in every direction. Andrew Johnson stood, confused by the sudden tumult. Then he understood the words that were being shouted and he gripped the porch railing, his face turned ashen.

"The President's been shot...the President's been shot."

For the first time in the country's brief history, a President had been shot, sitting in a balcony box at Ford's Theatre, attacked by crazed southern extremists.

"Eliza, Mr. Lincoln has been shot," Johnson said, staring at his wife, almost unable to comprehend the words he was uttering.

"Oh, my lord," she cried, dropping into a chair, tears forming in her eyes. "Is he dead?"

"I don't know. They seem to be shouting that he was shot while he and Mrs. Lincoln were at a private box enjoying a play. They haven't said anything about his being dead. My God, Eliza...we need to pray and pray hard that he survives. The nation needs Abe Lincoln to preside over our divided nation."

"Andrew," Eliza said, quietly, almost holding her breath. "If he dies you would become President."

The thought stunned them both. It was an unthinkable event. Neither wanted it to happen but...what if?

"I would be so ill-prepared," Andrew Johnson whispered, almost ashamed of uttering the possibility. "He needs to survive. Please, God, let our President survive this dastardly attack." Their prayers were unsuccessful.

Abraham Lincoln, 16th President of the United States, Savior of the Union, and freer of slaves, died days later. 'He is now one with the ages,' his friend, Edwin Stanton said, giving a moving eulogy.

Lincoln would be succeeded by Andrew Johnson, a man who had risen from poverty but whose philosophy was best summed up by his statement: "Damn the Negroes. I am fighting those traitorous aristocrats, their masters."

It was not with pleasure that Chief Justice Salmon Chase swore in the new President. Chase had been an early rival of Lincoln but after the 1860 election the two had become friends. After serving as Secretary of the Treasury in the President's Cabinet, shepherding the establishment of a national banking system and the issuance of paper currency that helped fund the war, and realizing he would never achieve his dream of becoming President, he resigned. In gratitude, the President was happy to grant Chase's request to fill an open position on the Supreme Court.

Chief Justice Chase was vocal in his opposition to slavery and not at all pleased that the man before him cared not one iota about the plight of the four million Negro ex-slaves now roaming the Confederacy without status. "This southerner wouldn't be fit to polish Abe Lincoln's spittoon," he'd said when he realized it would be his job to swear in the new President. He had donned his black robe for the obligatory ceremony with tears in his eyes.

"The war is over, thank God, and we must be united once again with our kin who were led astray," President Johnson intoned to the small crowd of well-wishers. It was difficult for the country to think about what lie ahead. They were in the midst of an emotional rollercoaster…elation and gratitude that the war had ended but crushing despair from the assassination of their beloved leader.

"I say to the Confederate leaders, punishment. I also say leniency, reconciliation, and amnesty to the thousands whom they have misled and deceived. I intend to confiscate the lands of these rich men whom I have excluded from pardon by my proclamation, and divide the proceeds, thereof, among the families of the *'wool hat'* boys, the Confederate soldiers, whom these men forced into battle to protect their property in slaves."

The new President's speech, reprinted in newspapers around the country, slowly awakened the public to the realization that Abe was gone. This was a new man, a Southerner, with new ideas. What no one understood was what it would all mean for the Negroes who were struggling each day to find work or something to eat.

Congress was in recess and would be for the next several months. The new President was free to interpret the rules for Reconstruction as he saw fit. Lincoln had urged leniency…an end to rebellion. But four million slaves were no longer property. They were now free but what did that mean? What were illiterate black men and women across the south supposed to do without an overseer to tell them? Where would they sleep…how would they eat and care for their families? A new integrated society had to be created and a shattered economy had to be rebuilt. Both the North and the South had used every resource at their disposal to fight the war and economic ruination scarred the landscape with more than 600,000 dead, or wounded. Five percent of the country's population of thirty million, one out of every twenty

Americans who had been alive and well five years earlier, was dead or seriously injured. Few families had been spared from tragedy.

Andrew Johnson rushed to implement his own policies. He appointed provisional governors in the defeated Confederate states and required them to call special conventions to draft new constitutions that abolishing slavery and renouncing secession. Once a state's convention ratified the constitution, it was permitted to send representatives to Congress and, thereby, be fully restored to the Union. All Southern voters would have to swear an oath of loyalty in order to obtain amnesty.

"I will not give amnesty," Andrew Johnson insisted, "to former federal officials who supported the Confederacy, graduates of the military academies at West Point or Annapolis who fought on the side of the rebels, high-ranking Confederate officers and political leaders, and any individual who had aided the rebellion and owned taxable property valued at more than $20,000. Any individuals who fell into these categories will have to apply personally to me for pardon and restoration of their political rights, and they'd better have a damn good story."

The provisional Governors Johnson appointed were a mixed lot but their views were generally consistent with those of the new President...punish the wealthy and begin to rebuild the economy. If that meant forcing the freed blacks...most of whom had been slaves with no rights, to return to their old masters on the farms and plantations, so be it. They needn't be property owned by these same masters, but they could certainly be share croppers. They would now be tied to the land in a new form of economic slavery. Someone needed to work, to till the soil, and to harvest the crops. It would continue to be a Negro work force...there was no one else. Good blacks, industrious blacks, he felt, would rise above the rest. It was the American way. And, to the new President, it wasn't the most critical issue that concerned him.

When Congress reconvened in December, most of the Senators and Representatives were appalled at the ease with which the Confederate states that had been so arrogant and shed so much mayhem were being allowed to return to the Union so effortlessly.

"You're thinking of passing high sounding Constitutional Amendments while that faux southerner sitting in the White House is appointing Governors that don't give a shit about blacks," Thaddeus Stevens shouted, his face turning red, his hands gesturing wildly. Stevens was a flamboyant speaker and the most dominant force in the House of Representatives. He had been reelected several times from his home in Lancaster, Pennsylvania and had devoted his career to urging a free public education for all now that slavery had been defeated.

"You know I want those southern bastards punished," Stevens said stridently. He had stormed across to the Senate building to the office of Lyman Trumbull, leader of the Senate Republicans and a long time friend of the new President.

Thaddeus Stevens   **Lyman Trumbull**

"Calm yourself, Thaddeus.   You'll have apoplexy," Trumbull urged.

"You ask me to calm myself but we lost good men from my Pennsylvania district, killed by Confederate grape shot. They fought to free the slaves and keep our Union together. Now the President's damn Governors are adopting laws like the ones Texas passed, defining anyone with at least one-eighth black ancestry to be inferior and subject to special laws.   Last month Mississippi passed their own Black Codes...laws that say Negroes must sign annual contracts. They can be heavily fined, hired out to whites, and all sorts of shit not applicable to their white citizens. In South Carolina their new laws refer to 'servant' and 'master' and define working hours for Negroes and their obligation for civility to whites. My people in Pennsylvania didn't don blue uniforms or leave their farms and have an arm blown off for that. It's slavery by another name and it is unmitigated bull crap. It's an insult to our deceased President."

Within weeks of reconvening, and with minimal resistance, Congress established a Joint Committee of Reconstruction to examine Johnson's policies. It quickly concluded that freed slaves were, more and more, being forced into their old lives and denied their rights. Those blacks, or the white scalawags who supported racial equality and objected, were maimed or killed. The Republican legislators were outraged. They voted overwhelmingly not to seat the newly elected Southern representatives or to recognize the newly reestablished state governments as having properly re-entered the Union. The Congress was not going to allow this new President to tarnish Abe Lincoln's legacy.

Hoping to continue to provide some direction for the traumatized southern Negroes, Congress passed an extension of the Freedmen's Bureau, a program enthusiastically supported by Abe Lincoln, fully expecting the President to sign it into law. This agency had successfully implemented a federal refugee program aimed at protecting and providing shelter and provisions for the displaced slaves as well as trials by military commissions of individuals accused of depriving Negroes and people of color of their civil rights. Managed by Union officers, the Freedman's Bureau helped set up schools and medical services. They supplied seed, or a mule, or basic farm tools at no cost so that families of blacks, once considered property, could now begin to support themselves. This was no time to end the effort.

Charles Sumner

To their surprise, Johnson not only vetoed the bill but he also attacked it as race legislation that would encourage a life of wasteful laziness for Southern blacks.   Congressional leaders were stunned.

"Lyman, what the hell is going on? Thaddeus Stevens is near having every blood cell in his body explode," Charles Sumner, one of the Senate's most vocal abolitionists, asked, as he stormed into Lyman Trumbull's office. "I thought you said we could work with this President. He's as bad as Jefferson Davis."

Charles Sumner was the scion of a Boston family and had, like many young Americans, lived in Paris thirty years earlier to absorb the culture and knowledge of the city. Negroes, he noted in a letter home, are treated with the respect their station in life deserves. It is clear that the racism we experience in our country arises from educational differences and not the darkness of their skin.

"I'm as surprised as you are, Charlie. I asked Thaddeus to be patient but we're all beginning to lose our patience. Lincoln picked Johnson as a running mate and it made sense at the time. The man vowed to support the President's policies and principles. I'm as perplexed as you are. Well, we certainly have enough votes to pass it over his veto. Damn shame. I've known Andrew Johnson a long time, but he's changed…and not for the better."

"Well, you run the Judiciary Committee in the Senate. Threaten him with impeachment. Get the son of a bitch in line," Sumner said, storming out with the same fury that had brought him into Trumbull's office minutes earlier.

Lyman Trumbull tried. He'd asked for an appointment to see the President but was repeatedly told the President was too busy. A few months later the Senate bill was passed over the President's veto and funding for the Freedman's Bureau continued. This time it was Andrew Johnson who was furious and determined to fight this obstreperous Congress that was opposing him.

The Senate, led by Senator Lyman Trumbull, and others, quickly proposed the 13th Amendment to the Constitution, legally ending slavery and involuntary servitude except as punishment for a crime. Slavery had never been outlawed in 'border' states. They wanted to make certain the Emancipation Proclamation was never interpreted as just a wartime measure. It soon began making its way through the state ratification process, made easier by the absence of the southern states that hadn't been accepted back into the Union.

"Let me talk to the President," Trumbull said again, trying to assuage his angry colleagues. "Maybe I can make him see reason. I've already tried several times without success but maybe overriding his veto or the likelihood of the 13th Amendment passing will get his attention."

"He's out of touch with his party and everyone who supported Abe Lincoln. Make him see that," Sumner pleaded.

*****

"Mr. President, thank you for seeing me," Lyman Trumbull said, respecting the office of the Presidency more than the political positions of the man standing in front of him, a former Senator with whom he'd shared many a sherry.

"Lyman, how are you? Eliza and I used to see more of you and your wife. We knew she had died and that you'd recently remarried."

"Yes. I was devastated by her loss, but two years as a widower was enough. Mary Jane has filled that void. A man without a good woman often loses his focus. But you know that. You and Eliza have always been a strong couple and wonderful parents."

"We try, but, really, it is Eliza that keeps the family functioning and morally directed. Now, what can I do for you today? I'm told the President can do a wide swath of things and I'm still learning what some of them are."

"I'll be frank. The people you have appointed as Governors in the South are making a mockery of your administration and our Republican Congress. Every state...every damn one of them is denying equality to the freedmen in their states. The damn Black Codes they're passing are creating new forms of slavery. Not one Republican in the Senate or House is willing to tolerate such blatant actions. It makes a mockery out of everything we fought for."

"Lyman, this is a country for white men, and by God, as long as I'm President, it shall be a government for white men. I'm willing to allow some Negroes to vote...if they can read and support themselves," he emphasized, "But equality with white men...never."

Johnson's statement was said with such frankness and stridency that it struck as a lightning bolt. These were the words and convictions of the men who had walked out of the Senate years earlier and their beliefs were anathema to those who opposed slavery and all it represented, and who had remained. Apparently, Lyman Trumbull realized, Andrew Johnson had been an exception.

"Andrew, forgive me, Mr. President, we've been friends a long time, and I desperately want that friendship to continue, but I must tell you I intend to propose a Civil Rights Act requiring racial equality in all matters. I shall also be submitting another Amendment, the 14th, to write such equality into our Constitution."

"Lyman, if the Congress passes such a law, I will veto it. Those matters belong to the states, not the national government. The southern states may have lost the war but they will be readmitted to the Union, and when they are, the national consensus will reaffirm that this is a white man's country. I'm sorry we disagree on such an important matter."

"As am I, Mr. President…as am I. Please give my best to your wife."

*****

The Civil Rights Act of 1866 that the Congress overwhelmingly passed provided full citizenship to all freedmen. Negroes who had once been slaves but who had been freed from bondage by the Emancipation Proclamation and the 13th Amendment would be chattels no longer. The Act declared that people born in the United States are entitled to be citizens, without regard to race, color, or previous condition of slavery or involuntary servitude. It also averred that a Negro citizen has the same right as a white citizen to make and enforce contracts, sue and be sued, give evidence in court, and inherit, purchase, lease, sell, hold, and convey real and personal property. Persons who denied these rights to former slaves were guilty of a misdemeanor and upon conviction faced a fine not exceeding $1,000, or imprisonment not exceeding one year, or both. Similar phrases were included in the 14th Amendment, just beginning to make its way through the various states.

As he promised, the President vetoed the bill. Within weeks, however, his veto was overridden and the bill became law. The breech between the President and his supporters widened. Andrew Johnson's programs were now more allied with those of the Southern Democrats than those of his own party.

The off year elections in 1866 were filled with rancor. The President campaigned and stumped for candidates, who agreed with him, but they were few, and he was ridiculed by the sparse crowds who came to see him. His message was ignored. A Republican landslide filled the halls of Congress with even more men who opposed the President. A storm was brewing. An attempt to impeach the President had been made in 1867 but it had failed. Unless the President ameliorated his attitudes, another attempt at impeachment was certain to be tried again.

"You've done what?" Lyman Trumbull asked.

"I said I've fired Edwin Stanton. I no longer have confidence in him," Johnson said, leaning back in his chair.

"You've fired a popular Secretary of War when we still have nearly a half million men in uniform and our cannons are still hot from battle. You fired a good friend of our recently slain President. Why not just declare war on the Congress?" Trumbull asked, his eyes bulging, astounded by the naiveté of the man he'd shared Senate chambers with.

The President had asked his former friend, and the Republican Senate leader, to join him for coffee at the White House. Trumbull's cup tipped over at what he'd just been told.

"The man was appointed by Lincoln," Trumbull raged. "Everyone thinks he's done a wonderful job. What about the Tenure in Office Act that Congress passed last year? It was very specific. Once the Senate advises and consents to a Presidential appointment, you can't fire that individual until they consent to a replacement and the Senate isn't about to approve of your firing the Secretary of War despite what you consider as undue pressure. He's a very popular man."

"My cabinet split 4-3 allowing the black residents of North Carolina to vote and own property. I was very clear. What North Carolina did wasn't our business. It was up to them to pass laws they felt appropriate for their citizens. Your friend, Stanton, then issues a public statement 'the opposition of the President to throwing the franchise open to the colored people appears to be fixed.'

"I will not have such disdain for my opinions within my own Cabinet. I don't need the son of a bitch, Stanton, rallying you, Sumner and Stevens and your extremist bunch. This is the White House...the Executive Branch. We don't cow-tow to the Legislative Branch. He's their eyes and ears into every decision we make. Last month I learned that he withheld information that a military tribunal had recommended the death warrant for Mary Surratt be cancelled and her sentence commuted to imprisonment. Instead, he convinced me to confirm the killing of someone I might have spared. It's my Cabinet and I need to be surrounded by those I can trust, and who support my policies."

"Forgive me, Mr. President, but your policies are creating a schism in this country the size of the Atlantic Ocean."

"That's what you and your friends say. I can say the same thing about them. My opinions are those of the majority of the white citizens of this country whether or not they are from states that have been readmitted to the Union."

"Perhaps, but until they are admitted to the Union and declare their loyalty for the laws of these United States, and not those of the defeated bigots of the Confederate States, their opinions are not relevant. If you persist in firing Secretary Stanton, I will not be able to stop another attempt at impeachment. Do you really want that?"

"Do as you must, Lyman. God will judge us all."

*****

In February 1868 the House of Representatives approved Articles of Impeachment against a sitting President for the first time in the country's history. On March 30th, Benjamin Butler stood before Chief Justice Salmon Chase and fifty-four

Senators to present the eleven articles that established the case for impeachment.

General Benjamin Butler

Benjamin Butler, overweight and bald, still carried the nickname given him by rebel forces around New Orleans. At that time he was General Butler, aka 'Beast Butler.' Some also called him 'Spoon Butler' for the reputation he'd acquired for pilfering the silverware from southern plantations. He was an opportunist and through the decades he'd changed from being a supporter of Jefferson Davis to Radical Republicanism. Now he would be at the helm of the effort to oust a sitting President. Most of the formal charges against President Johnson had to do with his alleged violation of the Tenure in Office Act...his firing of Edwin Stanton and his subsequent attempt to install Major General Lorenzo Thomas, one of Stanton's aides, as the new Secretary of War.

Johnson was further accused of giving speeches inciting the public against the Congress and of replacing Army officers who had been too aggressive in pursuing racial equality in the Southern states. He preferred to select men who worked with the establishment…his establishment that was committed to maintaining white leadership.

There were fifty-four Senators, two from each of the twenty-seven states in the Union. Two-thirds were required to convict. From the onset there were 35 votes for impeachment, 19 against. Only one of seven Republican Senators who had voted against impeachment was needed to support a guilty verdict.

Five of those dissenting Senators did so because they were convinced that the proceedings had been manipulated. The firing of Stanton was wrong, they believed, but the true reasons for the proceedings had to do with the President acting with increasing belligerence against racial equality. He was fighting the Congress at every turn. Lyman Trumbull, a sixth dissenting Republican, agreed with their conclusions, but he didn't believe the President's actions rose to the levels of 'high crimes and misdemeanors' required by the Constitution. The seventh dissenting vote was that of Edmund G. Ross, Senator from Kansas.

Ross had been a Senator for barely two years. He was a newspaperman before accepting a commission as a Major in the Union Army. When the sitting Senator from his state committed suicide, the state's Governor appointed him to complete the man's term. Ross was a man whose feelings were difficult to discern. His shiny black hair, sharply parted, and held in place by heavy quantities of pomade, gave him a stern look. He rarely smiled...he was a very private person.

Senator Edmund G. Ross

"Senator Ross, you have a visitor," his secretary announced.

"That's no visitor, that's my friend. Come in, Tom."

Thomas Ewing, Jr. walked into Senator Ross' office and the two greeted one another warmly. Ewing had been Ross' superior officer for more than a year during the war and the two became close friends through the months of battle. Once the war ended, Ewing returned to the practice of law and successfully defended three of the men accused of Lincoln's assassination. The men were convicted, and imprisoned, but they were not hung.

"What brings you to these hallowed halls, Tom?"

"I'm hoping to convince you to side with those voting to acquit the President. Impeachment is a serious offense and he's not guilty of anything more than having a serious spat with Congress."

"I don't care a fig about Stanton, or the Tenure Act, but he continues to thumb his nose at our efforts at Reconstruction. You fought against the evils of slavery. We saw men standing next to us in battle suddenly fall from a Confederate bullet. Johnson is shredding everything we fought for...and the policies of Abe Lincoln he swore to uphold. "

"Edmund, he's the President. You're a Senator. You're both allowed to have your points of view. That's what elections are for. Let the voters decide at the next election what path they want to take. Don't usurp that authority under false pretenses.

"Would you rather have Benjamin Wade as President?" Tom Ewing continued. "He's a leading voice among the Radical Republicans and, as President Pro-tem of the Senate; he'd be next in line. He's in the Senate shouting for the President's impeachment. But it is quite obviously self-serving. He'd benefit most from a guilty verdict that would oust Johnson. It could be the beginning of another Civil War. Your choice isn't whether to impeach an intemperate President.

It's whether you want to install someone else in the White House...someone you know holds really extreme views."

"I'll think on it. I will," Ross promised.

"I can't assure you that continuing to dissent from voting for impeachment will be popular. The good people of Kansas may not reelect you."

Benjamin Wade (as a young man)

"I'm sure they won't. Jayhawkers have long memories," he laughed. "Thomas, thank you for coming! I understand the importance of my vote. Six of my associates have made their decision and whether I cast my vote yea or nay, I am stuck with a responsibility I would rather have avoided."

Edmund Ross left his office at the end of the day, turned up his coat collar, and strolled along the Potomac. He sat down on a bench and watched three pigeons fighting over a small piece of bread someone had thrown. It was late in the afternoon and the path grew more crowded as workers left their offices and hurried home to their families, unaware of the precarious issues that might affect their lives. There was

no one with whom he could share his thoughts. Tom Ewing
had put it succinctly. This was his responsibility. He disliked
Andrew Johnson, all the more for the admiration he'd had for
Abe Lincoln. The two men, one from Illinois and the other
from Tennessee, both who rose from the humblest of
beginnings, were the alpha and omega of what Presidents
should represent. He glanced at a newspaper someone had
left behind. There on the front page was an editorial with a
small headline: *'Andrew Johnson is innocent because Ben Wade
is guilty of being his successor.'*

Ross read the next paragraphs. *'Benjamin Wade is bright. He
is tenacious. But he is too autocratic for the majority of the
Republicans to follow. He has made too many enemies.'*

Two days later, when the votes were tallied, the result
remained 35-19, one short of that necessary for impeachment.
Edwin Ross had voted against impeachment and, without his
single vote, the President was acquitted. Senator Ross served
out the balance of his term but he lost his attempt at
reelection. Kansas voters did have long memories. He
returned to the newspaper business in Kansas.

*****

In the fall of 1868 General Ulysses S. Grant, victorious
leader of the Union Army, was elected President of the
United States. At Christmas, President Andrew Johnson, as
one of his final acts, granted unconditional amnesty to all
Confederates, no longer requiring loyalty oaths to the United

States. It was a final act of defiance against those who had opposed him.

Andrew Johnson and his family returned to Tennessee. He ran for the Senate in 1868 but the emotional wounds surrounding his failed impeachment trial were too raw. Too many people still remembered, and he lost. In 1874, however, he was returned to the Senate and became the only former President to ever serve in that body.

V

THE FAILED ANNEXATION OF SANTO DOMINGO i.e. THE DOMINICAN REPUBLIC

"We lost 37 seats in the election," Grant shouted from his White House office, "Thirty-seven damn seats in the House and six seats in the Senate. Every time a Confederate state is readmitted to the Union, it elects Democrats. If this keeps up, we're going to get our asses whipped in the '72 elections and every damn election after that. He, and his Vice-President, Schuyler Colfax, had stayed up late into the night receiving telegraphed election results from around the country. It was an off-year...no exciting Presidential race but plenty of people upset nevertheless. The two men were nothing alike. Ulysses S. Grant had always been a soldier, a West Point graduate, and a fearsome General. He had taken the battle to the enemy, seen the fires of hell, and returned victorious to a grateful nation. His Vice-President was a quiet man, a few inches taller than the President, more temperate in his drinking Colfax was well-liked and a gifted speaker. He was the consummate politician who had risen in the political ranks as a Whig and a friend of Horace Greeley, famed publisher of the New York Tribune, the most influential newspaper in the country. While Greeley remained a friend of Colfax, his newspaper had become increasingly critical of the revelations of corruption within Grant's administration. The two men scanning the steady flow of wires brought into

102

the office did agree on one important thing, however...the evils of slavery and the need to bring the Negroes into an integrated society.

President Ulysses S. Grant

Vice President Schuyler Colfax

"It could have been a great deal worse," Colfax noted. He had left his post as Speaker of the House during Andrew Johnson's Presidency to run with Grant on the Republican ticket. "It isn't uncommon for the party that won the Presidency...us, to lose seats in the subsequent election."

"I don't give a crap about what's common. You know as well as I do that the whites in the southern states are scaring off the blacks and making it difficult, or impossible, for them to vote. If we allow that pattern to continue, the Democrats will have a head start in every election from now on and, if you don't mind, I'd like to get reelected in 1874."

Colfax was not unfamiliar with politics or what happened to men when they took on the mantle of the Presidency. It had certainly changed Andrew Johnson. The minimally educated man from Tennessee, thrust into running the country when President Lincoln was assassinated, went from a proponent of Abe's temperate and conciliatory policies to his own programs. He chose to ignore the Congress and damn near got himself impeached and thrown out of office. Now Colfax began to wonder whether he wasn't seeing the same inclinations in the man he was talking to, storming around the room, and refilling his whiskey glass for the third time in an hour.

"At least the economy is steaming along," Grant said with considerable pride in his voice. "We're building a network of railroads across the country from the Atlantic to the Pacific. And, we're bringing in nearly ten million people a year to our country. Sometimes I think we're emptying out the cities of Ireland, Germany, and the rest of Europe. Yes, Schuyler, our nation has a great future ahead of it."

"I'm glad you're enthusiastic, Mr. President, but I urge caution. Anytime our economy has grown too quickly, something happens to burst the bubble. People are investing their savings in these railroads and I fear their enthusiasm isn't justified. If we have problems with the economy it could mean serious unemployment would exist just when the next election is going to be held and that would mean trouble."

"You worry too much, Schuyler. We have our political enemies on the run, and if we can get political stability in the Confederate states, the Republican Party can direct this country for the next few decades."

The President stopped to stare out the window at the front lawn. There was no moon and it would have been pitch black except for a sky full of stars. The sun's first rays of the morning were another few hours away. He stifled a yawn and took another deep sip of his whiskey. I like being the President, he thought. I liked running the Army but I think this job suits me even more. He heard Colfax clear his throat from the other side of the room and wondered how long he'd been lost in thought.

"The Freedman's Bureaus are doing a good job across the old Confederacy, but there aren't enough Union soldiers down there to offset all the Klan and white paramilitary groups that roam and harass blacks trying to get their lives started," Grant said as he refocused. "We need a new direction. We need a program that convinces those bastards to treat the Negro labor force that grows their cotton and tobacco with more civility, instead of the abuse they seem to enjoy inflicting," he paused, letting his cigar move from left to right, continuing to chew the end, "Those Southern fuckers continue to treat their black citizens like cow dung."

"If the plantation owners thought they were going to lose their workers, they might treat them better," Colfax noted, warming to the conversation. His face suddenly lit up.

"What if we resurrect the idea of annexing one of the islands in the Caribbean, like Cuba, where blacks are free?" he asked.

"Not Cuba, despite their desire to get out from under Spain, I'd just as soon not launch another war. But, what about Santo Domingo? It's larger than Cuba and we've had discussions with them on and off for years," Grant asked, his forehead furrowing as he dropped himself onto a couch, careful not to spill a drop from his glass.

"It's been tried before, dating all the way back to President Buchanan in the '50's. The southern states blocked it then and they'd probably block it now."

"I'm not sure. Today we have a national sense of 'manifest destiny,' a need for naval bases and an energetic public attitude that this country can be anything it wants to be. Damn it, we need to try again, and this time it needs to succeed."

*****

A small U.S. Navy frigate plied smoothly through the waters of the Caribbean on its way past Cuba. A school of dolphins kept pace, dancing along the white caps. On board was Orville Babcock, President Grant's personal secretary and envoy, and General Rufus Ingalls, an old military friend of the President who had been responsible for setting up the Union Army's quartermaster facilities during the recent war as it deployed its divisions across the states that comprised the Confederacy.

"I'm better on land than the sea," Ingalls complained. If I'd wanted to have my stomach upset all the time, I'd have joined the Navy."

The island of Hispaniola lay less than a hundred miles southeast off the tip of Cuba, less than eight hundred miles off the coast of southern Florida. After an arduous and dangerous journey across an uncharted ocean on his first voyage, Christopher Columbus and his men landed on the north side of the island, wet and tired. One of his three caravels, the Santa Maria, had barely made it to land. It sank fifty yards off shore. They were greeted tolerantly by the Taino Indians who inhabited that part of the island and after resting, and taking on what fresh supplies the island could offer, Columbus departed with his two remaining ships, leaving forty of his men to establish a colony. When he returned a year later, all his men were dead. He could get no explanation but it was easy to believe the Indians had killed them. Rather than land and face the same outcome, he sailed around to the south side of the island and established the first permanent European community in the Americas. The site was not far from Santo Domingo, capitol of the country where the American frigate was now heading.

As the frigate tied up, Babcock and Ingalls stood at the gangway, staring down at a man smiling up at them. They walked down, glad to be back on dry land.

"Buenos dias, señores. Welcome to Santo Domingo. My name is Juan Duarte."

"Are you any relation to Juan Pablo Duarte?" Orville Babcock asked.

"He was my father. You knew him, señor?"

"I met him once, a long time ago. I know how much he did to help Santo Domingo gain its independence from Haiti."

"Si, es verdad. *(It's true.)* As a younger man, he and others formed a secret patriotic society called *La Triniteria* and successfully fought several pitched battles with the Haitians to gain our independence. He was wounded in the shoulder and later he was exiled as a revolutionary. Tragically, he died last year in Venezuela. It was an ignominious ending for a very brave man."

"I'm sorry."

"Señores, estoy muy alegre que ustedes aquí, *(I'm very happy you are here.)*" Duarte said, refocusing his attention on this official greeting that he had been given as his responsibility. "Presidente Baez is waiting for you at the palace."

"Nosotros, tambien," Babcock replied.

"I didn't know you speak Spanish," Ingalls said.

"Very little. Duarte said he was glad we were here and I said that we were as well."

"Does Baez speak English?"

"Quite well, I think."

"Good," the General said, "Otherwise I'd be spending my time nodding, having no idea what was going on."

Buenaventura Baez stood at the top of the stairs of the Presidential Palace, an ornate, but badly weathered, building left over from the original Spanish occupation. He was surrounded by several other very official individuals, a few smiling but most looking quite serious. Baez was distinguished looking with dark, well-coifed hair. He wore a tight-fitting suit, several elaborate medals pinned neatly to the front of his coat.

Buenaventura Baez

Baez' mother, a freed slave, had inherited a fortune from her husband. This allowed Buenavanture to be educated at Europe's finest schools. He spoke multiple languages fluently but preferred to keep all public discourse in Spanish. He was now in his fourth term as President, none consecutively, due to the erratic nature of the island's politics. His current term had begun in 1868.

He greeted both his visitors with a warm, European-style hug, followed by an American hand shake. It took several minutes for all the introductions to take place and the group to retire to a small conference room.

"I have made rooms available at my residence," Presidente Baez said. "I hope that will be acceptable. It will give us more opportunity to talk. I am grateful that President Grant has sent such esteemed men."

"He sends his regards, Presidente," Orville Babcock replied diplomatically.

"Tomorrow I have arranged for you to tour some of our island. We have many natural resources and with American capital and American markets both countries can benefit."

"I would also like to see more of your harbor. A permanent port for American ships will have to be part of any arrangement we negotiate," Ingalls said.

"Por supuesto, General Ingalls…of course…we understand the desire of your Navy to have a permanent base in the Caribbean. I have always agreed with what your President Monroe said fifty years ago…this hemisphere wants no interference from European powers and with an American umbrella spread across the area, they would be most reluctant to be aggressive."

Babcock ignored what seemed like an arrogant tone in his associate's voice.

"You have many blacks in your country, I understand," Ingalls said intently. He was on an important mission and getting the facts was more important than diplomatic niceties. "Do you find that to be a problem?"

"No entiendo," Baez said. "How do you mean, a problem?"

"In our country some of the white citizens are uncomfortable working alongside our black citizens."

"Si, ahora entiendo *(now I understand)*. You fought a war for this and ten years later it is still a problem in your country, particularly in your southern states. In Santo Domingo such a problem does not exist. Here our Spanish who never left, our Haitians who stayed, and our blacks all get along. We have many problems, señor, but skin color is not one of them."

*****

"Good morning, señores. I hope you slept well and enjoyed your breakfast. I am Roberto Salazar, and I will be your guide for the day. I have been instructed to have you back by sunset so that you and our Presidente Baez can share a dinner together. Will that be satisfactory?"

Babcock and Ingalls smiled, nodded, and followed the tall, well-built man to three waiting horses. His skin was bronzed from the sun but it would be difficult to determine from which of the island's many cultures he had descended. They were pleased, however, that their guide spoke English as well as either of them.

"These horses are descended from those the Spanish Conquistador brought to the island. It is the only thing of value they left us," he laughed easily. "I have taken the liberty of providing hats for you. The sun around Santo Domingo can be quite intense. Forgive me if I tell you things you already know. Our city dates back to Christopher Columbus and his brother, Bartholomew. The Spanish arrived in force twenty years later. Ours was the harbor where all the Spanish galleons landed going and coming from, stealing the gold and silver from the well-developed societies of the Peruvian Incas and the Mexican Aztecs. It made our city wealthy and you can still see some of the ornate buildings the Spanish built. All that ended when our city became home of the English pirate, Sir Francis Drake. Does this bore you?" he asked.

"Not really," Orville Babcock said agreeably, watching throngs of people milling around, bringing their produce to the city. Women walked, while their children lagged behind or scampered ahead. Some men walked or pulled small donkeys loaded with farm produce. Faces were panoply of brown shades ranging from latte to near-black.

"It is a market day today. We have two each week. People bring things they grow on their small farms to the city to sell. The land is quite fertile."

"I haven't seen any blacks with pronounced African features," Ingalls noted. "You know, wide spread nostrils, large lips, tight curly hair...that sort of thing."

"You're talking about slave features from the first group brought out of Africa. Slaves haven't landed in Santo Domingo for more than a hundred years and any that stayed married and blended with our people."

The men rode through the low hills that climbed away from the harbor and stopped to rest.

"That is one hell of a harbor," General Ingalls looking down approvingly at the large deep water bay, well-sheltered from the prevailing winds. It was the sort of place the American Navy would find quite useful. Surrounding the harbor was heavy green vegetation interspersed with straw covered cottages. It was a lush island that, from a distance, could easily be mistaken for a paradise.

Dinner that evening was limited to Baez and the two Americans. There were several influential groups who would have been delighted to know the details of what was being discussed. They wanted their island of Santo Domingo to keep its distance from larger countries who well understood the advantages of controlling such an island. These men wanted no interference in their nation's future.

Santo Domingo should belong to Santo Domingans, not Americanos, or Spaniards or anyone else. Presidente Baez had wisely chosen to keep discussions of annexation by the United States very private.

Baez selected a cigar and rolled it between his thumb and forefinger, filling his lungs with the aroma before handing the carved wooden box to his guests.

"From our friends in Cuba. Their tobacco is unsurpassed. Now, let's talk seriously," Baez said, falling comfortably into an overstuffed chair. "If your country annexes Santo Domingo you get a harbor and natural resources. We get protection from the Spanish, and, most recently, the Dutch. They keep sending ships and making overtures. We will never be strong enough to remain independent. We need to be allied to someone larger and your country would be an ideal partner. Furthermore," he added, after inhaling deeply from his cigar and blowing a well-formed circle into the air, "You will bring capital into our country and we will have new markets for our products."

"That all sounds wonderful, Presidente Baez," Orville Babcock said, enjoying his first Cuban cigar but trying to avoid coughing from the unfamiliar heavy tobacco. "Your country is politically unstable. Why are you so sure the people will see such a close relationship with the United States the same way you do? President Grant has no interest in stationing American military troops on your soil if your people are unhappy with the relationship you are proposing."

"I have asked them. More than 80% favor such an arrangement."

Babcock laughed. "And I'm sure you worded the question in a very favorable way."

"Por supuesto (of course)," the island's President laughed.

*****

Orville Babcock and Rufus Ingalls were ushered into President Grant's office.

"Welcome back, gentlemen. We are anxious to hear your report." The President was in a gregarious mood as if someone had just told a joke. His hallmark glass of whiskey was still in his left hand as he rose to shake hands. "This is George Robeson, Secretary of the Navy, and you all know, Schuyler Colfax, my Vice-President. I want them to hear what you have to say."

"I think we were both favorably impressed," General Ingalls began. "Particularly with two things you asked us to consider, the harbor and their racial situation. Their harbor is large, deep, and angles in such a way as to mitigate some of the force of any hurricane that might trouble them in their annual rainy time of year. Racially, they have none of our problems. Of course, they don't have a lot of whites on the island but those who are there mix well with all the locals. Racism the way we know it here just isn't present."

"It would be good for us to have a permanent port in the Caribbean," Robeson offered. "Having American ships patrolling the Caribbean makes sense, particularly if we ever decide to build a canal across the Isthmus of Darien through Central America."

"We got their signature and approval of the Treaty your people provided," Babcock chimed in. "And, which we brought with us. It contains the provisions we'd all discuss. We annex Santo Domingo and we agree to pay them two million dollars for Samana Bay, the site our naval engineers selected. All we need now is for the Senate to approve it. Presidente Baez is most enthusiastic. He believes if we don't step in, the Dutch might and if one European power steps in we all felt it would open the door for other nations to follow. Keeping the Western Hemisphere away from Europe is in all our interest."

The men smiled. Only a few outside the room knew that Babcock and Ingalls had carried a Treaty with them. President Grant hoped that having it already signed by President Baez might smooth Senate passage.

*****

At a separate meeting in Boston, Frederick Douglass and Charles Sumner sat at a small table in a café overlooking the Charles River. Frederick Douglass was likely the most famous Negro in America, certainly the most influential. He had aged. He had already been fighting slavery and injustice for more than three decades but the full head of grey hair and the wrinkles around his eyes did nothing to diminish his influence or his fervor. He was a dazzling orator who had escaped from being a slave thirty years earlier and matured to become an ardent, and vocal, abolitionist. He was the nation's conscience when it came to Negro civil rights.

Charles Sumner represented Massachusetts in the Senate. He was a Radical Republican, a member of that most liberal wing of his party. Several years earlier he had been beaten viciously with a cane by an angry South Carolina Congressman who was demanding no Federal interference to his state's right to own slaves. It took Sumner nearly three years, and multiple surgeries, to regain his strength. It was he and other Radicals who had defeated Andrew Johnson's attempts to weaken Reconstruction efforts. The two men now sitting together were soul mates, both working toward nothing less than racial detente.

Charles Sumner

Frederick Douglass

"Tell me about this Santo Domingo proposal of the President," Douglass said. "Is it real or just a ploy to get the public's mind off all the scandals in his Administration?"

"It's real. One reason is the Navy…a permanent base in the Caribbean…Monroe Doctrine and all that. The other reason is race and that's why I thought that you and I should meet."

"I was sure that subject of the plight of the Negro was somehow involved. Please, continue." Frederick Douglass knew exactly what the President had in mind. The few Negro Congressmen who served in Washington had been privy to inside information. Grant hoped that many free blacks, seeing new economic and social opportunities in color-blind Santo Domingo, would relocate, and the Southerners, concerned that their cheap labor force might leave, would be forced to offer concessions in terms of civil rights to the vast number of freed slaves now trapped in the degrading bondage of sharecropping. It was a rather simplistic, but optimistic, view of human nature but any idea that furthered opportunities for Negroes was an idea that Douglass would support. He remembered, too bitterly, the stories of Negro families trying to leave the South after the Civil War for better lives out west or in the north only to be stopped by white thugs forcing them to turn around. The plantations needed bent backs to pick the cotton and harvest the tobacco. To those hoodlums, blacks would always be 'niggers'…inferiors, meant only for heavy lifting and stoop labor.

"The President wants to reopen the debate of annexing the eastern part of Hispaniola...Santo Domingo," Sumner continued. "The bottom line is that he has evolved a well-intentioned, but circuitous, logic that he can use this new land to improve the situation for southern blacks. It's naïve at best."

"Charles, you say naïve, but perhaps a more appropriate word would be creative. We both agree that the present situation cannot last. At some point the north will weary of the permanent stationing of Union soldiers in southern states and when they leave, there will be bloodshed. This large island country is under populated and Negroes who live there are treated as equals. I'm not saying it's perfect but it is something and anything is better than the status quo."

Sumner stood and walked to the open window overlooking the Charles River. He took a deep breath of the cool air and quietly watched two sail boats tacking to and fro for several minutes until they were out of sight.

"I remember when Senator Windom wanted to make some place like Oklahoma into a home for ex-slaves. It never passed the Senate. The South doesn't want a mass exodus of blacks. They need that cheap labor. What I want to do is give them a better life, a chance to go to school, raise their families, and vote for the type of representation they want."

"We want the same thing," Frederick Douglass nodded. "I just believe this idea of Grant's might work."

As debate on the treaty was about to begin in the Senate's Foreign Relation Committee, chaired by Charles Sumner, the Senate was seating its first Negro member. Hiram Revels, an educator and minister of the African American Episcopal Church, from Mississippi.

Hiram Revels

He had been appointed by his State's legislature for a plethora of impressive accomplishments but his credentials were objected to by other southern Senators. These whites had no interest in having a black join their exclusive club. Senator Sumner brought the debate to an end with a stirring speech.

"The time has passed for argument. Nothing more need be said. For a long time it has been clear that colored persons must be allowed to join our body as Senators," he said to the entire body.   Without further discussion, following loud applause by the Republicans who dominated the Senate, they voted 48 to 8 to seat Revels.

The Treaty to annex Santo Domingo was another matter. It pitted long time allies against one another.

"Frederick," Charles Sumner said, "This is one of those rare times when you and I are on different sides of an important issue. I find that voting with the Democrats a rare and most uncomfortable predicament but I cannot support this Treaty."

"I regret the situation, as well," Douglas answered. "The President wants this Treaty. I want this Treaty. And, if they were permitted to join this debate, the majority of Negroes in our country would also want this Treaty."

"You are right about the President and you may be right about the Negroes but it will not solve their problems. If we support this expansion," Sumner argued, "It will dilute our efforts to work for equality among American Negroes. The people of Santo Domingo may share skin color with many of our citizens but they are of a different culture. Establishing a colony for persecuted Americans, of any color, is not the direction we should go."

"American Negroes need an alternative," Frederick Douglass countered. "Caribbean blacks are free without threats to their lives if they vote or seek elective office. They share in the same education and opportunity for their families as others in their country. It would give Southern Negroes an alternative. It would force Southern governments to ensure that their citizens, black and white, share equally in their state's future or lose them to live elsewhere. Santo Domingo has asked for a place in our Union. They are eager to be protected under the umbrella of the United States. It can benefit them as it benefits our people."

"Gregorio Luperon, a popular leader in Santo Domingo, has sent me a long letter voicing his opposition to the treaty," Sumner retorted, waving a three page letter over his head. "All citizens of that country are not supportive of this Treaty, regardless of the claims of Presidente Baez and President Grant. They don't want to lose their national identity. They want to trade with the United States, nothing more."

*****

Newspapers around the country printed the speeches President Grant was making daily in support of the Treaty. 'National interest,' 'Protect our shipping and trade routes,' 'Annexation would force Cuba and Puerto Rico to abandon their policy of allowing slavery.'

Americans barely followed the arguments. Neither those supporting annexation nor those opposing it, was able to generate public heat and support for their position. The political wrangling continued on its own, with diminished enthusiasm. The population of the country was more concerned with the dangerous sagging of the economy.

On March 15th, 1869 passage of the Treaty to Annex Santo Domingo failed by one vote. Nineteen members of the Senate had chosen not to vote. They could see no political advantage to commit to a position. The result was 28-28. Had the Treaty received a simple majority…one more vote, it was believed enough of the uncommitted Senators would have voted to give the Treaty the two-third majority needed for its passage. Everyone who had argued so fervently was exhausted, not least its champions, Frederick Douglass and Ulysses S. Grant. Charles Sumner, who had fought so hard to defeat its passage, was relieved but too tired to rejoice. His single vote had influenced others to withhold their support and block passage. Had he found himself morally able to support the treaty, there was no question that his vote would have provided the impetus to annex the island.

Three years later El Presidente Baez was toppled from government. A year after that he returned to his island's Presidency, only to be thrown out again. Santo Domingo became the Republic of Santo Domingo…the Dominican Republic, but political instability continued to haunt the country and stifle its growth. One can only conjecture on what annexation to the United States would have produced for either that country or the freed slaves of the American confederacy.

VI

THE DISPUTED PRESIDENTIAL ELECTION OF 1876 – THE END OF A DECADE OF SUMMER; THE BEGINNING OF A CENTURY OF WINTER

America was gripped in the worst economic depression it had ever experienced. The expansion and optimism that followed the Civil War had overinflated the economy and in September 1873, following the collapse of Jay Cooke's New York financial empire, it burst. The flamboyant and influential Cooke had helped finance the Civil War but the war had now been over nearly a decade and things had changed. There were too many railroads, too much track, too many factories, and too much farm goods. The shortages of the four year internecine strife between the north and the south had been absorbed and the supply of goods now being produced far exceeded demand. Produce was rotting in the fields, stacked rails, waiting to be laid, had begun to rust, and families ebullient the year before, were now wondering where their next meal would come from.

Whether the scandals of President Ulysses S. Grant's administration worsened the economic chaos gripping the nation can only be conjecture.

In the 1874 mid-term elections concerns over the economy and government scandals swept Democrats into control of

124

the House of Representatives for the first time in decades. dozen infamous events of corruption came to light beginning with Black Friday…a collapse of the New York Stock Exchange following stories of how speculators had manipulated the gold market. Other investigations revealed stories of corruption by Grant appointees at the New York Custom House. Meanwhile, other appointees earned millions from bribes awarding land grants and government contracts.

Jay Cooke

*****

Several months earlier, in the late morning of a warm July day in 1873, several men gathered at the Cooper Union, a small private college, located in New York's East Village. The college had been funded by Peter Cooper, a wealthy inventor and philanthropist who believed in wide-spread, low cost education. Technically the college's name was the Cooper Union for the Advancement of Science & Art but everyone just referred to it just as the Cooper Union. Carriages arrived separately from both uptown and downtown including Wall Street and Park Avenue. Samuel Tilden's carriage arrived from the office he continued to maintain at his old law firm, despite the substantial amount of time he was currently spending in Albany.

"Glad you could join us, Sam," Peter Cooper intoned.

"Nice to be invited. How's the steam engine business?"

"Terrible! We're still suffering from the damned depression. There isn't much demand for my engines if no one is building factories or producing steel. These lethargic business conditions have been going on for more than a year and show no sign of turning around. I may have to go back in the glue business that made me my first million."

"Not likely, but if all that crap going on around Grant doesn't settle down, people will trust government less than they do now.'

Political cartoon of Boss Tweed

"Between Grant's scandals and Tweed's bull shit, can you blame them?"

"All these investment bankers who repackaged the tin-plated lies that Jay Gould and his friend, Daniel Drew were spewing are going under as well. I understand Drew is thinking of filing bankruptcy."

"I've heard that. He got so badly fleeced by Fisk and Gould over that worthless Erie railroad stock that he's nearly penniless. I'm sure Tweed got his share of the dirty profits. But if anyone deserved to get taken, it was Drew. For years he thought nothing of cheating his own investors."

"Anyway, the others are already here. Let's get the meeting started," Cooper said, once Tilden and the others, all old friends, had shaken hands.

"Gentlemen, thank you for coming. I won't waste your time with preliminaries. Most of you know why we're here. We need to be able to make sure that a Democrat gets elected President in 1876 and that New York helps pick the right man. To do that we'll need to get our own house in order and that means cleaning out Boss Tweed, the crooked judges he has on his payroll, and the rest of his cronies. Sam Tilden has made a good beginning from his position in the Assembly. I want your support in electing him governor next year."

Samuel J. Tilden, a lanky, wealthy lawyer with impeccable family credentials, became Governor of New York in 1874 and proceeded with cleaning out the corruption and bribery that had infected much of his state. With his success he was catapulted to national popularity and at the Democratic convention in St. Louis in June 1876, he was nominated for President on the 2nd ballot. Given the stench of Grant's Republican administration, the Democrats were optimistic they could finally recapture the White House. All the states of the Confederacy had now been readmitted to the Union and were fervently against the Republican establishment that had defeated them in a bloody four year war that had destroyed their economy. Furthermore, these same people, all Republicans, continued to demand a racial equality that was anathema to them. Yes, the Democrats had good reason to be optimistic.

Samuel J. Tilden

Rutherford B. Hayes sat in his overstuffed leather chair and leaned back, staring out his window that overlooked Columbus, Ohio's Capitol complex. He was thinking about the events of the past few weeks. He had been elected Governor of Ohio three times and he had grown comfortable with executive responsibility. He was good at it and he thought he'd been a good Governor, a responsible leader. He stared at the small photo his desk of his mother and sister. The three of them had struggled together when his father died. His mother had been a pillar of strength, raising two children by herself. He knew, if she'd lived this long that she'd be proud of him and what he'd achieved.

"Governor, can I get you anything?" Wilbur Hutchins, his secretary and close advisor asked. "I haven't really had a chance to congratulate you since you received the Republican nomination for President. All of us are sure you'll win handily."

"Well, it took them until the 7th ballot to make their decision, but, yes, I'm very pleased."

"Arranging to have the convention in Ohio certainly didn't hurt, clever move."

Rutherford B. Hayes

"It's going to be a battle," Hayes said, folding his hands over his ample mid-section. He thought of himself as portly, not fat, a sign of prosperity. His long full-face beard was increasingly peppered with gray but he had the same energy he'd had twenty years earlier. "Grant is leaving us with a legacy of villains who have been feeding off the public trough for years and the voices of the southern Democrats keep getting louder. No, this election is going to be close."

"I doubt you're going to get much support in the south," Hutchins said, shaking his head. "There is that one plank in the platform...'the complete protection of all its citizens in the free enjoyment of all of their constitutional rights,' is pretty clear and it isn't going to sit well with the white citizens of Mississippi or the Carolinas."

"It was meant to be as clear and unambiguous as possible. I don't care or myself but if I lose this election, I do worry about the poo colored people of the south. The white citizens of the old Confederacy will have no reluctance in keeping the Negro population from voting or just killing them whenever they feel the urge." The message of each party was simple. The Democrats demanded an end of corruption to bring prosperity back to the country and, more importantly, an end to Federal interference in the states...a return to 'Home Rule.' The Republicans tried to distance themselves from the scandals that plagued Ulysses S. Grant's his last two years...years that continued to rupture the economy. They preferred to insist that the Democrats, particularly those in the South, were traitors and didn't deserve to lead the country. The Federal government needed to continue 'Home rule' to ensure racial equality in the old Confederacy.

"Not every Democrat was a Rebel, but every Rebel was a Democrat" rang as a battle-cry from north to west. Democrats responded that Republicans keep *"waving the bloody shirt"* of a war that ended a decade earlier. *"Stop corruption!"* *"End Home Rule!"*

Rutherford B. Hayes campaign train that criss-crossed across the southern states was a tiring and frustrating exercise, but one that was necessary, if he had any chance of taking the election from the more popular Governor Tilden. When he reached Louisiana, he was joined by Governor Warmouth and the colored Lieutenant Governor, C.C. Antoine.

"You certainly have a beautiful state, gentlemen," Hayes explained. He had never been to New Orleans and there was a certain thrill in visiting a city that had such a wonderful reputation for debauchery.

"How's the sentiment here?" he asked.

"Dangerous sums it up," Warmouth offered. "The Democrats across the state have made a conscious effort to either threaten or kill the blacks. Sometimes they just smooth talk some of those folks into thinking that they are their friends. In one parish they've paid off a local preacher and invited the blacks to join them at barbeques and picnics. In other parishes the members of the local white gun clubs ride through the countryside at night singing:

"A charge to keep I have; a God to glorify.

If a nigger don't vote with us, he shall forever die!"

Folks hear that and most decide to stay away from the polls. Another threat is that they'll lose whatever job they've got and won't be able to support their family. Sharecroppin' ain't much of a life but it does keep a roof over their head and some food on the table for their families."

"That's terrible," Hayes said, shaking his head as the three men walked along the quay watching the ships that had come through the Gulf to meet the paddle boats that had traversed south along the Mississippi River from Natchez and points north. This confluence is what made New Orleans such a vit l t rac e hub.

"What ar : v e doing to counteract the Democrats?" Hayes asked.

"We h vi n' been idle," Antoine said. He was a handsome man, clear-eyed, who spoke English with a delightful French lilt. "We travel across the state registering blacks and coloreds and, whenever possible, we get the help of the Union soldiers to fight the white demagogues."

"You're the third man of color to be Lieutenant Governor, aren't you?"

"Yes, Governor Hayes, I am. But I tell you very clearly that if you don't win this election, I will certainly be the last. Sam Tilden and the Democrats that will get elected with them will destroy every multiracial institution in this state. There will be no protection for blacks and the poor, illiterate ones who are share cropping will be no more than indentured servants."

Lt. Governor C.C. Antoine

"Tell me about share cropping. Doesn't it give the workers a share in the profits instead of being slaves owned by a white master?"

"In theory, but it rarely works out that way. Croppers are tied to the land by a contract. They live in shacks, they're forced to buy most of their food at the plantation store and since most can't even do their numbers, they're just told at the end of the year what they earned and what they owe for rent and supplies. They're lucky to break-even at year's end and when cotton prices are low, like they have been these past few years, they're kept in debt. If they try to leave, armed white posses catch them and beat or kill them. No, governor, they're as tied to that land the same as if they were still chattel."

"I've heard the same in other states," Hayes said sadly. "Paramilitary groups such as the Klan, the Redshirts in Mississippi and the Carolinas, and the White Camellias here in Louisiana, cajole and kill blacks and whites sympathetic to candidates supporting equal opportunity.

But by Election Day the voters had come to believe that Samuel Tilden's record of reform was more likely to return the country to prosperity and they voted their pocket books. Economic opportunity was of greater importance than continuing the status quo.

When the votes were counted, Samuel Tilden had won 51% of the popular vote, 4.3 million of them. Rutherford B. Hayes had received 49% of the popular vote, just over 4.1 million. There was cause for the Democrats to celebrate. Tilden also had amassed 184 electoral votes to Hayes' 165. It would only take 185 votes to determine the election... but there were 20 electoral votes in question. Contested election disputes in Louisiana, Florida, and South Carolina, the only states in which Negroes outnumbered whites, put the election in doubt. Who was going to make a determination of which electoral slate was valid? What to do? The country was frozen. This had never happened before.

Democrats shouted *"Tilden or War!"* A Kentucky Congressman declared that an army of 100,000 men was prepared to march on Washington if Tilden was denied the presidency. The Constitution was mute on how such matters should be resolved...by Congress...by the Senate...by the Supreme Court. Each party was certain that any choice favored their opposition.

In January 1877, fearing widespread bloodshed throughout the land, Congress quickly passed an act which was immediately signed by the still President Grant. It established an Electoral Commission to resolve the disputed electoral slates. This group would consist of fifteen members: five representatives selected by the House, five senators selected by the Senate, four Supreme Court justices specifically named in the law, and a fifth Supreme Court justice selected by the other four. The most senior justice was to serve as President of the Commission. Whenever two different electoral vote certificates arrived from any state, the Commission was empowered to determine which slate was the most valid. The Commission's decisions could be only overturned by both houses of Congress.

Political party balance was essential to ensure the public's willingness to accept the outcome. The country was divided and a renewal of violence between the Hayes and Tilden factions loomed as a potential threat. There were to be seven Republicans, seven Democrats, and one Independent, Justice Daniel Davis, Associate Justice of the Supreme Court. There were three Democrats and two Republicans from the House, two Democrats and three Republicans from the Senate, joined by four Supreme Court Justices who, it was believed, were also split two-two in their leanings. Davis, as the fifteenth member, would head the commission, and, being an avowed Independent, would likely cast the critical deciding vote. It was a commission that satisfied no one but promised the most equitable resolution of a complex situation.

Daniel Davis' family had settled around Bloomington, Illinois when there were only a few families in the area. Daniel followed the path of his forbearers in attending Yale Law School. He was an early supporter of Abe Lincoln, another hick from Illinois, and Davis became active in the new Republican Party, although his spirit and easy temperament made him popular with those across the political landscape. Daniel loved to eat.

Justice Daniel Davis

He could sit with his friends for hours, laughing, drinking, and eating. Now well into his sixties, he weighed over three hundred pounds. He was independent of thought and believed by both Republicans and Democrats to be the perfect choice to be the fifteenth man on the Electoral Commission. He could help resolve the unique conundrum facing the country and for the moment a kind of serenity existed while the nation held its collective breath.

*****

Six heavy set men crowded around a table in a small private dining room at the Hay-Adams Hotel.

"Daniel, congratulations on being appointed to the Electoral Commission," Gustav Andrews said, putting heavy dabs of butter on a roll. Andrews was a leader of the Republican legislature in Illinois. He and Davis had been law partner's decades earlier.

"Are you so sure congratulations are in order?" Davis replied. "Whatever decision the Committee makes will bring cries of fraud from half the country."

"Your reputation for being an independent thinker will serve you well." The speaker, sitting on Judge Davis' left, was John Beveridge, Illinois' Governor, who had traveled clandestinely to meet with the justice.

"And why have you come, John? You don't often leave the state and I'm sure you've got more interesting things to do than have dinner with me."

"You underestimate your charm," Beveridge laughed. "I enjoy watching you eat. One day I expect you to put salt on the table and china and take a chomp out of them."

"I prefer oysters and a good French wine. Now, stop the small talk. What's the reason for this dinner?"

Beveridge, Andrews, and the others looked at one another and smiled.

"Once this commission business is done, the Legislature has appointed you to the U.S. Senate. We're hoping that you'll step down from the bench and take your place in the Upper House, representing the good people of the State of Illinois."

Voices stopped and everything froze, as if in a frieze, as the visitors waited for the reaction of their long-time friend, Justice Daniel Davis, soon to be Senator Davis. His friends didn't know him as well as they thought, however.

"Thank you," Davis said softly. He ended the evening shortly the reaft r, foregoing his traditional cigar. He was both pleas d an l insulted and he needed time to sort through his feeling . T ese were his friends and he thought they knew him. App arently he thought wrong.

In an at emp to influence his decision, the Republican-controlled Illinois legislature had appointed Judge Davis to the U.S. Senate, believing their action would ensure his support for Hayes. They didn't want their friend's independent mind set to tilt in the wrong direction. It didn't work. Two days after being told of the Governor's offer Judge Davis shocked everyone by resigning from the Supreme Court and the Electoral Commission. Knowing that their intent had been to both reward him and influence his decision, he knew he could no longer be independent. He immediately accepted his new appointment to the Senate.

The hope that the Commission would reach an impartial decision, once again, hung in uncertainty and there were few options left that might satisfy both factions. The March Inauguration Day couldn't legally be delayed. Another Supreme Court Justice was their only viable option.

The Presidency might now depend on Justice Joseph Philo Bradley, white-haired, respected, and thought to be the most neutral, and only remaining, option.

Justice Joseph P. Bradley

Joseph P. Bradley had never sought the spotlight. He would have happily remained at New Jersey's Millstone Academy after graduating from Rutgers but he was persuaded to pursue a career in patent and railroad law.

The effort made him wealthy. Bradley had always been a member of the Republican Party and supported their programs quietly. He was appointed to the Supreme Court in 1869 and, with Daniel Davis' unforeseen decision to resign, he would now be the fifteenth, and likely, deciding vote on the Electoral Commission.

The Committee began its meetings without fanfare. They were faced with deciding the outcome in the three disputed southern states as well as Oregon, where the Democratic governor claimed the selected Republican elector was ineligible despite statewide results favoring Hayes. The initial decision to give one vote to Tilden and two to Hayes was ultimately nullified and the Commission awarded all three electoral votes to Hayes.

What to do with the three southern states that had submitted conflicting results was more contentious. Claims of fraud and threats of violence were everywhere...always against black and Republican voters. One issue was the design of the ballots. To aid illiterate voters, parties used symbols to represent their candidates. The southern Democrats had cleverly used Republican symbols, such as a picture of Abe Lincoln, to lure innocent voters. In Florida the Republican sitting Governor opposed the newly elected Democratic Governor. In South Carolina electors simply claimed they represented the popular vote. These assertions were rejected by that state's Republican election board.

Louisiana had struggled with the country's most acrimonious and violent election. Militant racist groups such as the White Camellias and hooded Klansmen had ridden across the state maiming and lynching. 'The Negro is divinely created to be the servant of the White' was emblazoned on banners. It was a belief widely held and unfettered by the end of the Civil War a decade earlier. A year earlier a New Orleans convention to enfranchise more blacks turned into a riot that killed or wounded nearly two hundred angry whites and blacks. More than two thousand more were attacked in the weeks leading up to the election. In an 1868 local parish election Republicans outpolled the Democratic candidates. Eight years later, however, in that same parish, after widespread intimidation, the Republicans failed to get a single vote. Threats and violence had been victorious.

What would Judge Bradley do? The onset of another Civil War might rest on the decision he and the committee would make. It was clear the remaining fourteen members were voting consistent with their long time party affiliations. That would make the vote 7-7. Bradley had to make a decision and the import weighed heavily on his shoulders. He was not comfortable being in the eye of the hurricane. His entire career had been unassuming. Someone had to come forward to resolve this matter.

*****

"Rutherford, we need to put this impasse to an end." Samuel Jackson Randall, Speaker of the House and a Democrat from Pennsylvania, was among a small group of men who had come to Ohio to meet with Governor Hayes. Randall was young, with wavy, black hair and thought to have a reputation for being popular with the ladies.

The others, sipping Kentucky bourbon and pacing nervously around the room were three Governors: Francis Nicholls, newly elected from Louisiana, Richard Coke of Texas and Wade Hampton of South Carolina. They were 'Redeemers,' a new small wing of Republicans who supported the ouster of scalawags, Union soldiers, and carpetbaggers from southern states and from the Republican Party. Nicholls was in the midst of his own disputed election and would never be affirmed unless the Presidential dispute was resolved in favor of Hayes. With the overwhelming number of southern whites supporting the Democratic candidates, these men feared for their future.

"That's easy," Hayes smiled. "Declare the Republican slates from the disputed states to be valid and make me President. We all know the Democrats in your states kept the Negroes away from the polls."

"Whether they did or didn't is irrelevant at this point," Nicholls pointed out. He was the youngest man in the room, not yet fifty, but he wore a full beard that helped give him a more mature appearance. "We need a solution that satisfies enough hot heads on both sides to keep the peace. We have urgent economic problems to solve. In case you've forgotten, our country is suffering from a deep financial malaise."

"You must have something in mind," Hayes said, standing, and walking slowly over to the decanters on the side board. "Can I refill anyone's glass?"

His wife, Lucy, would be very upset if she knew her husband was offering alcohol to her guests. She was head of the local Temperance movement. In deference to her he now limited himself to a glass of wine.

"If you want to be President, you'll have to do something to assuage the southern states. You'll need to end Home Rule and withdraw all the Union troops," Wade Hampton blurted out.

Hayes laughed. "Tell me you aren't serious. I take the troops out and we might as well not have fought the Civil war."

"If you tell him to, Grant will withdraw the troops. You won't be blamed. And slavery is over...it isn't going to return," Coke said, speaking up for the first time.

"That's bull shit and you all know it," Hayes said, returning to his chair, and taking a large swallow of his drink. His face had gotten red with anger. "Those Confederate assholes will still be fighting that war into the next century. They will never acknowledge the concept of racial equality."

"Rutherford," Randall said quietly, a condescending tone creeping into his voice, and hoping to lower the level of rancor rising in the room, "Bull shit is in the eye of the beholder. Grant will withdraw the troops, Justice Bradley and the Electoral commission will certify enough disputed electors to give you the election, and you'll be President."

"Does Sam Tilden know about this?"

"It doesn't matter. The country will be better off. What do you say, Mr. President?"

Hayes sat quietly. It wasn't easy to ask a man to give up his principles. He had left the Whig party a decade earlier because of his convictions regarding the evils of slavery. But he was also a politician and it was even more difficult to ask a man who had given his life to public service to walk away from becoming President of the United States or to preside over a divided nation as Lincoln had done.

"I'll let you know in the morning," Hayes said, taking a deep breath.

"We need to know..." Richard Coke began angrily, when he was stopped in mid-sentence by a heavy arm on his shoulder.

"That will be fine, Rutherford," Sam Randall said quietly. We'll reconvene at nine if that's acceptable."

The four men left and Hayes sat quietly, pondering his options.

It was near midnight when Hayes donned his coat, and left his office. Wilbur Hutchins had offered to stay but Hayes needed to be alone. He needed time to think and he enjoyed the chilly evening air along the river. The moon reflected on the water and he took a deep breath as he meandered along the path. He was alone, not just physically, but spiritually as well.

There is more to this than whites and blacks, he knew. There's the economy. If we don't get it moving again, the entire country will continue to suffer. There is that Texas and Pacific Railroad project that Jay Gould and his business cronies want to build that connects Texas and Southern California. It could mean jobs and trade across the southwest, but only if the Federal government can provide the project a financial subsidy. I could do that if I were President, he said to himself.

He was torn. He knew he'd make a good President, and he did so want the job. Would the whites treat the blacks reasonably or would everything Abe Lincoln and the north fought for disappear in a whiff of smoke? He'd been shot in the knee and the arm in separate battles as a Union officer. He'd seen too many men die. He wanted to believe they had all served and died for an important cause. Now he was being asked to put that cause at risk.

He walked over to the Methodist church where he and Lucy attended services every Sunday. The door was open. He sat in the front pew. It was quiet. Maybe God would talk to him. Help him decide what do. He wasn't sure the Almighty talked to mere men but at the moment he'd try anything. An hour later, as the sun was rising, he returned to his office.

*****

The rest is history. Rutherford B. Hayes accepted the *'Devil's Compromise'* and became President of the United States. Justice Bradley, as the fifteenth member of the Electoral Commission, had been happy to validate the Republican slates from the disputed states. The Commission voted 8-7, but it was a formality. The issue had already been resolved. Rutherford B. Hayes, Governor of Ohio, had become President of the United States by a single vote. He was assured that the new mantra of *'separate but equal'* for blacks and whites would replace the umbrella of protection the army had provided since 1865 and that racial tensions would actually decrease. He chose to believe it would be true but he knew in his heart that he had condemned southern blacks to an uncertain future.

Ulysses S. Grant, in one of his final acts as President, began the withdrawal of 200,000 Union soldiers from the states that had formed the Confederacy. The decade of racial progress that had seen the enactment of new state Constitutions and educational opportunities for those who had slaves, a true movement toward racial equality, would come to a grinding halt.

In 1877, a few months after taking office, President Hayes made a tour of the South and made the following off-hand statement in an interview with a reporter:

> *I considered the situation of things in the South; how impossible it seemed to restore order and peace and harmony; saw the violence and bloodshed at their elections; how white Republicans as well as black, were shot down during their political contests, and I asked myself why is it, and how long this must continue. Those men down South –the white educated citizens—are as good men as you or I; they are Christians; not thieves nor cutthroats; nor bandits, yet they see things and tacitly approve them, if they do not take part in them. Why is it, and how long will they continue? …that one word, war, solved in my mind the problem of the South. The South was still at war and, perhaps, if we remove the causes of war, there would be peace, and ultimately, harmony and prosperity.*

His hopes were not to be achieved and, in his later years, he wrote extensively, apologizing for his naiveté. Meanwhile, the following decades saw new laws passed by all the states that had formed the Confederacy effectively eliminating voting by Negroes. Jim Crow laws, Ku Klux Klan violence, and racial segregation became the norm. Negro education disappeared...economic opportunity disappeared. *'Separate but equal'* turned out to be always separate, but rarely equal, and the Federal government ceded all decisions in these matters to the states.   Decades of fear, intimidation, and economic slavery would continue to exist well into the mid-20th century.

VII

THE ANNEXATION OF THE PHILIPPINE ISLANDS

The sinking of the USS Maine in Havana Bay, Cuba, had been enough to stoke American testosterone into declaring war on Spain. The temptation had been building, encouraged by larger and bolder headlines from the Hearst and Pulitzer newspapers competing for circulation. *Freedom for Cuba! End Spanish imperialism!* Theodore Roosevelt had written to a friend: "In strict confidence . . . I should welcome almost any war, for I think this country needs one." It was spring 1898 and the memories of the death and bloodshed of the Civil War now resided in the memories of an older generation.

The Bureau of the Census had declared that the internal frontier was closed; the country had achieved its *'sea to shining sea,'* its manifest destiny. With an insatiable desire for further expansion, many businesses had already begun to cast covetous looks overseas. The severe depression that began in 1893 had ebbed. Farms and factories had excess capacity. Even a growing population couldn't absorb everything our fertile and industrious country was able to produce. New overseas markets for American goods might relieve the problem and assuage our desire to expand. American muscle had already demonstrated its willingness to engage the navy beyond our shores. That same Navy had helped overthrow the established monarchy in Hawaii to protect the sugar and pineapple plantations of Sanford Dole and others. The Army had sent troops into Nicaragua to protect American economic interests. Both adventures had been successful. The country was ready for something more. Captain A. T. Mahan of the U.S. navy, a popular propagandist for expansion, exerted his influence. "The countries with the biggest navies would inherit the earth," he said. "Americans must now begin to look outward."

America had grown bigger, bolder, and more arrogant. And, as General Leonard Wood and Teddy Roosevelt readied troops to land on Cuban soil, a US Naval armada, under command of Commodore George Dewey, defeated a smaller Spanish fleet in the Battle of Manila Bay. Spanish control of the large island chain was over but, like Cuba, there was a strong ongoing movement for independence by local patriots.

The desires of the Philippine people for independence began well before the arrival of American forces. In late 1896 and through the heavy rains of early 1897, an insurgent group, led by Emilio Aguinaldo, made major inroads against better equipped Spanish forces. The brief war ended in a truce but the Spanish army still wanted to capture the Filipino insurgents and punish them. They were forced to retreat to Hong Kong. Commodore Dewey met with Aguinaldo.

"Señor Aguinaldo, I am happy to meet you," the American Commodore said, rising to greet the Filipino leader and shake the hand of this man he had heard so much about. He offered the shorter man, wearing jungle fatigues, a cigar and led him out onto a balcony overlooking Kowloon.

Commodore Thomas Dewey

General Emilio Aguinaldo

"We have a strong enough navy to defeat the Spanish fleet," Dewey continued, chomping off the end of his cigar and spitting it onto the street below. "But it will take your rebel army to defeat their land army. Can you do that?"

"Of course. We are fighting to free my country. Since it is likely your army will conquer Cuba, the Spanish forces will have little stomach for a prolonged war."

While Dewey's forces attacked from the sea, units of the rebel army fought to control the cities. Within a month the Filipino army surrounded the island's capital, Manila. Afraid of excessive violence, Dewey ordered the rebels to stay out of the city in the same way Cuban rebels were not allowed to enter Havana.

"The Americanos have tricked us. They mean to take over our country and subjugate us just as the Spanish did. We will not trade one conqueror for another," Aguinaldo said furiously.

"I hereby proclaim the establishment of the Republic of the Philippines, an independent nation," Aguinaldo shouted from the steps of the old Spanish governor's mansion in front of thousands of supporters. Guns were fired into the air, people roared '*ole*' until their throats hurt and tears flowed openly.

"I urge the American government in Washington and the other nations of the world to support our independence."

But both the United States and Spain refused to recognize the islands as a new country. Spain, unable to reinforce its distant possession, agreed to surrender and depart from the islands. As Christmas 1898 approached, the Spanish empire that had ruled the oceans for three centuries collapsed. America and Spain signed a treaty. Spain sold Guam, Puerto Rico and the Philippine Islands to the United States. Emilio Aguinaldo, his Army, and the Philippine people were outraged. The new island republic declared war to defend its independence. Having helped defeat the Spanish, and exhausted from their years of war, they now undertook to fight the bigger, better equipped American military.

Domestically, the United States was in the middle of a renaissance. It was enjoying a new vitality fueled by innovation. Automobiles were beginning to be seen sharing dirt roads with horses and carriages. Electric lights were illuminating cities and homes. Prizes were offered to the first men who could fly a heavier-than-air craft. People were able to talk to one another over wires. It was all very exciting. The war with Spain was over and America had proven its might. Cuba was just offshore, laden with burgeoning opportunities for investment. It was also smaller, both in size and population. It was simply a 'friendly' neighbor. The Philippine Islands were another problem entirely, one not so easily defined.

The islands that comprised the Philippines were 6,000 miles from the Pacific Coast, nearly 9,000 from the American capitol in Washington, D.C. where their fate would be decided. Adding to the dilemma was their population and geographic complexity. Many of the islands were densely populated. In total there were more than seven million people spread across 7,100 islands, including more than forty different ethnic groups speaking more than eighty different languages or dialects. Cuba was a single piece of land with all its inhabitants speaking a single language. The Philippines enjoyed no such homogeneity.

The United States now faced a war it didn't want with people it didn't want to fight. The Philippine-American War was brutal. These people wanted their independence and America found itself fighting a land war on unfamiliar soil...damp, hostile terrain the Army had never experienced. The Filipino Army, though small and poorly armed, was supported by an overwhelming number of the local population.   American soldiers, unable to distinguish combatants from civilians, attacked Filipino troops and innocent non-combatants alike. More than 200,000 Filipinos died of war-related causes. The island of Luzon lost nearly ten percent of its population.   It took more than sixty thousand American soldiers three years of island hopping and jungle warfare to achieve control of the islands.   The entire foray into Cuba had taken only one hundred days.

President William McKinley

President McKinley, who was lauded for the country's success in Cuba, was conflicted on what to do with the islands. He told a group of ministers visiting the White House the problem he faced:

> *The truth is I didn't want the Philippines, and when they came to us as a gift from the gods, I did not know what to do with them. I sought counsel from all sides, Democrats as well as Republicans, but I got little help. I thought first we would only take Manila; then Luzon, then, perhaps, other islands as well.*
>
> *I walked the floor of the White House night after night until midnight; and I am not ashamed to tell you,*

gentlemen, many times I went down on my knees and prayed to Almighty God for light and guidance. One night, quite late, it came to me this way -- I don't know how it was, but it came:

1) We could not give them back to Spain -- that would be cowardly and dishonorable.

2) We could not turn them over to France or Germany, our commercial rivals in the Orient -- that would be bad business and discreditable.

3) We could not leave them to themselves -- they were unfit for self-government -- and they would soon have anarchy and misrule over there worse than Spain's was; and

4) There was nothing left for us to do but to bring them into the bosom of Mother Liberty. We would educate the Filipinos, and we would uplift, civilize, and Christianize them. By God's grace we would do the very best we could by the. We would treat them as our fellow men for whom Christ also died. And then I went to bed and went to sleep and slept soundly.

It was rationalization at its worst.

At home, the debate intensified. Those who supported annexation and American foreign expansion included Teddy Roosevelt and Henry Cabot Lodge, the influential Senator from Massachusetts.

"All you have to do is look west," Roosevelt championed. "Beyond the Philippines lie China and the vast untapped markets of Asia. Diplomatic efforts are already underway in China to have American companies build railroads across China. We will be exporting American steel and know-how. Meanwhile the cattle ranches of Texas, the farms of the Great Plains, and the factories of the northeast are enthralled with the untapped potential that satiates all our imaginations."

Very little of these dreams actually existed, but the fantasies helped shape the nation's policy toward the Philippines. Foreign expansion was vital to the growth of the country. Now John D. Rockefeller and Standard Oil entered the picture. As the 19th century turned toward the 20th, oil and petroleum products had grown to become second to cotton as the leading product we produced and exported overseas.

Expansionists were further emboldened by the American military. Just as they had supported the Cuban adventure to secure control of the Caribbean, they now saw the Philippines' value as a fueling and resupplying station for U.S. ships; as well as a springboard for expansion to China. Some religious leaders echoed the President's sentiments…'*we are duty-bound to educate, domesticate, and 'Christianize' the islands.*'   They ignored the fact that most Filipinos were already Catholic. Newspapers painted the Filipinos as primitive 'savages,' unable to govern themselves or to defend themselves against threatening European powers. The shouts to control the Philippines grew to a cacophonous roar.

But there were also those individuals who opposed the war and the blood that was being shed. This varied cluster included William Jennings Bryan, Mark Twain, and Andrew Carnegie.   They held meetings, wrote editorials, and sent petitions to Congress. Their voices galvanized hundreds of thousands. Those same voices, however, were ignored by millions of Americans more concerned with their daily lives. Mark Twain wrote:

> *I thought it would be a great thing to give a whole lot of freedom to Filipinos, but I guess now that it's better to let them give it to themselves. We have pacified some thousands of the islanders and buried them; destroyed their fields; burned their villages, and turned their widows and orphans out-of-doors; furnished heartbreak by exile to some dozens of disagreeable patriots; subjugated the remaining ten millions by Benevolent Assimilation, which is the pious new name of the musket; we have acquired property in the three hundred concubines and other slaves of our business partner, the Sultan of Sulu, and hoisted our protecting flag over that swag.*
>
> *And so, by these Providences of God -- and the phrase is the government's, not mine -- we are a World Power.*

A soldier from Nebraska wrote: *'We came here to help, not to slaughter, these natives...I cannot see that we are fighting for any principle now.'*

Racial attitudes became part of the national debate.

"We do not need to urge or absorb another non-white race to join the U.S.," the Senator from Mississippi said on the floor of the Senate, to the applause of most other southern delegates.

"The idea of uplifting the Filipinos is hypocritical when our Federal Government has failed to protect the rights of black citizens," Negro leaders shouted from the pulpit and black-owned newspapers.

Included in the American Army were four black regiments. Two of these were stationed in the Philippines. It was easy for these Negro soldiers to establish rapport with the brown-skinned natives on the islands. Too often the Negro soldiers were taunted by the white troops who used the word "nigger" to describe both them and the Filipinos. A large number of black troops deserted during the Philippines campaign, preferring the racial acceptance of the island's natives. The Filipino rebels often addressed recruiting efforts to "The Colored American Soldier" in posters, reminding them of lynchings back home, asking them not to serve the white imperialist agenda against other people of color.

Another group, smaller in numbers, also began to voice their opposition to annexation. It consisted of a coalition of businessmen, intellectuals, and politicians who opposed traditional colonialism. They advocated a free trade policy through which American products and know-how could be sold throughout Asia and other undeveloped areas without taking on the huge burden and responsibility of annexing the islands.

But the influential New York *Journal of Commerce*, which had always argued against military intervention, preferring the expansion of free trade, suddenly changed its position to one of support for annexation. They watched as European powers began to ravage a weakened China and its nearly half billion people. They saw a market for surplus American products speeding to China through a Canal dug across Nicaragua supported by an enlarged U.S. Navy, and they urged the support of the American public and its representatives. They saw the Pacific as a small body of water where American ships filled with American products could ply the ocean in an endless economic bounty.

The Treaty of Paris between Spain and the United States needed ratification from the American Senate, presided over by President McKinley's Vice-President, Garret Hobart.

"You did a good job, Garret," McKinley said, putting down the parchment treaty.

Vice-President Garret Hobart

"Thank you, Mr. President. It took nearly six months of negotiations but we got Spain to recognize the independence of Cuba and assume their debt. They also ceded the islands of Puerto Rico and Guam to the United States as war reparations. The most difficult part of the discussions was convincing them to cede the Philippine Islands to us in exchange for a payment of $20,000,000. That's a real bargain. I think they realized their empire was gone and their navy would be in no position to protect islands half way around the globe populated with a hostile people."

"A masterful job... Garret... a masterful job. Now let us hope that we can convince the Senate."

It was a blustery, biting day in February 1899 when the Senators removed their coats and scarves, downed a quick brandy to remove the chill, and entered the chambers. A full complement in the Senate would be 88 but illness and absences reduced that pool to 84. A two-thirds vote would be required. The vote of 56 Senators would be needed for passage. Senator Beveridge, a Republican from Indiana opened the dialogue for annexation:

> . . . Just beyond the Philippines are China's illimitable markets. . . We will not renounce our part in the mission of our race, trustee of God, of the civilization of the world. . . Where shall we turn for consumers of our surplus? China is our natural customer. England, Germany and Russia have moved nearer to China by securing permanent bases on her borders. The Philippines gives us a base at the door of the entire East. The Filipinos are a barbarous race, modified by three centuries of contact with a decadent race, the Spanish...It is barely possible that 1,000 men in that entire archipelago are capable of self-government in the Anglo-Saxon sense. The Declaration of Independence applies only to people capable of self-government. How dare any man prostitute this expression of the very elect of self-government peoples to a race of Malay children of barbarism, schooled in Spanish methods and ideas? And you, who say the Declaration applies to all

*men, how dare you deny its application to the American
Indian? And if you deny it to the Indian at home, how
dare you grant it to the Malay abroad?*

"President McKinley supports annexation and he
demanded that his Secretary of State and I negotiate for
nothing less," Hobart added. "His *Proclamation of Benevolent
Assimilation* is quite clear…Americans have a responsibility to
educate, civilize and uplift the conditions of the Filipinos."

"We fought for it, we have earned it," Senator Henry Cabot
Lodge shouted.

Mark Twain rebutted, *"I have read carefully the treaty of Paris,
and I have seen that we do not intend to free, but to subjugate."*

Five of the forty-seven Republican Senators were
outspoken anti-imperialists. The most outspoken was George
Hoar, an elderly, soft spoken man from Massachusetts. His
speech galvanized those who opposed the treaty:

> *You have sacrificed nearly ten thousand American
> lives — the flower of our youth. You have devastated
> provinces. You have slain uncounted thousands of
> the people you desire to benefit. You have established
> re-concentration camps. Your generals are coming
> home from their harvest bringing sheaves with
> them, in the shape of other thousands of sick and
> wounded and insane to drag out miserable lives,
> wrecked in body and mind. You make the American
> flag in the eyes of a numerous people the emblem of
> sacrilege in Christian churches, and of the burning
> of human dwellings, and of the horror of the water
> torture. Your practical statesmanship which*

disdains to take George Washington and Abraham Lincoln or the soldiers of the Revolution or of the Civil War as models, has looked in some cases to Spain for your example. I believe--nay, I know--that in general our officers and soldiers are humane. But in some cases they have carried on your warfare with a mixture of American ingenuity and Castilian cruelty.

Your practical statesmanship has succeeded in converting a people who three years ago were ready to kiss the hem of the garment of the American and to welcome him as a liberator, who thronged after your men when they landed on those islands with benediction and gratitude, into sullen and irreconcilable enemies, possessed of a hatred which centuries cannot eradicate.

There would not be enough remaining Republicans to get the Treaty accepted. The Senate Democrats would be able to muster enough votes to defeat it...but political considerations and the Presidential election of 1900 would be held soon. The Republicans were sure to renominate William McKinley and Garrett Hobart. The Democrats would likely nominate the same man they had selected in 1896, the silver-tong Orator and populist, William Jennings Bryan.

In that election Mark Hanna, a Republican strategist pulled together diverse groups and raised enough money to outspend the Democrats 5:1. The upcoming election would be even more difficult. The economy had been reenergized and the 'good little war' against the Spanish had been won.

"I want you gentlemen to vote for the treaty," Bryan said, sitting on his bed at the Hay-Adams hotel. He was surrounded by eight Democratic Senators, standing, sitting, leaning against the wall.

Senator George Hoar   **William Jennings Bryan**

"You have to be kidding," Stephen White said. He was an unapologetic critic of expansionism and a Senator from California. "I have petitions here from Andrew Carnegie and our ex-President Grover Cleveland, supporting rejection of the treaty. I plan to read them into the Congressional Record tomorrow."

"William, we can't support the treaty. Not at this point. Not after opposing it so openly," George Hoar added. "This treaty is wrong...plain bad thinking. We'll end up just as bad as the European countries we've been so critical of. It's only been three years since they all met in Berlin and divided up the entire continent of Africa. Now, if they want to sit on China's doorstep, let them.   That's not what America represents. The Filipino people deserve their independence."

"I don't disagree," Bryan said, "But we aren't going to win the upcoming election unless we have a strong issue to campaign on and that issue has to be imperialism. There are a lot of people who are against this treaty. If we defeat it now the issue goes away. If the treaty passes, we campaign hard on its evils and we vow to give the islands their independence if we get elected."

"If we allow it to pass, and then lose the election, then what?" Hoar asked.

"Then the seven million people of those islands will have been royally screwed and their Spanish masters will have been replaced by American imperialists...us," Stephen White said, shaking his head. A week later the Senate voted on the treaty. It passed by one vote, the vote of a reluctant Stephen White. He had finally been pressured to support Bryan's scheme.

The treaty was passed and the United States annexed a very unhappy island population.

Senator Stephen White

More than a half century and two world wars would pass before the islands would gain their independence. The election of 1900 was a rout...a lopsided victory for the Republicans. William Jennings Bryan's hopes were dashed once again. Garrett Hobart died suddenly and McKinley chose the energetic and ebullient hero of San Juan Hill, Theodore "Teddy" Roosevelt as his running mate. Stephen White regretted what he'd done. With his single vote, he'd damned the hopes of seven million citizens to control their own destiny.

VIII

AFFIRMATIVE ACTION

Fifty years ago...a century after the Civil War, more than two hundred million Americans continued to struggle with inequities in race, and individuals from vastly different backgrounds ended up connecting in ways none of them could have foreseen.

A young boy, blond-haired, white, with a warm smile and a surfer's tan, was growing up in an upper middle class enclave of southern Florida. Allan Bakke, born just before the onset of World War II, enjoyed his family, his friends, running along the white sand, and squashing the large red palmetto bugs that plagued his house and school.

Allan Bakke

He graduated from Coral Gables High School as a National Merit Scholar but money in the family for college was limited. Allan got accepted as an Undergraduate at the
166

University of Minnesota. He was able to defer his tuition costs by joining the school's ROTC program.

After all, it was only appropriate. His uncles had served in World War II. Other friends, older, had fought and died in Korea. Allan excelled in school. Four years later he graduated with a 3.51 grade point average, a strong B+. But now as the late 1960's and the country was engaged militarily in Vietnam.

Allan Bakke had his ROTC obligation to fulfill. Rather than await his enlistment orders, he joined the Marines Corps, trained at Perris Island, and was shipped with his unit overseas. He served with distinction in Vietnam. As he struggled to understand the carnage around him, his interest in medicine evolved. He came to have the utmost respect for the field hospitals and medics who had to function under adverse conditions. By the time he was discharged, he had decided what his career goals were. He wanted to be a doctor. He began sending out applications to a variety of medical schools. This was the career he had chosen. He was bright, enthusiastic, and he had served his country. He anticipated no problem. Twelve schools, including the University of California-Davis, one of his top choices, rejected him, primarily because of his age. This was 1973 and Allan Bakke, already thirty-three, was late to begin medical training. He would be a decade older than his class mates. On the positive side, however, his grades were good. On the MCAT, Medical College Admissions Test, he scored in the top 3%. By all criteria other than age, he was fully qualified.

*****

Three thousand miles to the west and a decade after Allan Bakke was born, Patrick Chavis, a Negro, came screaming into the world of the black housing projects of Compton, California. It was the early 1950's and tract homes across Southern California were being built to house the influx of Americans moving west to enjoy the Sunshine state's new prosperity and warm climate. Most of Compton's families weren't sharing in the new bounty, however.

Patrick and his four siblings were raised by a single mother who worked as a beautician to support her family. She was forced to supplement her meager income with welfare. Patrick's father was gone and financial help from him would never exist. But the Chavis family was God-fearing and his mother hoped for something better for her children. Every Sunday, Lila Chavis would dress her children in clean, ironed clothes, and walk the three blocks to the AME Church. The children learned to sit quietly and listen to the Minister preach on sin, the evils of the Devil, and the glory of Jesus Christ.

In California Patrick's world was the bleak streets of Compton, the cramped quarters of their apartment, children in his school that had less than he did and the shininess of the church. In Florida Allan Bakke was getting ready to enter middle school. The lives of the two boys couldn't have been more different. One, white, upper middle class, the other black, lower middle class, was struggling in a school where the goal of a college education was often more a dream than a reality.

Patrick was ambitious, and bright. His mother had instilled a sense of morality in her children. Avoid the temptations of drugs and gangs that prowled Compton's streets. He graduated from Compton High School with decent grades. In Compton, simply getting a high school diploma was quite an accomplishment. His mother and siblings sat on the folding chairs at the school's small graduating ceremony and Lila cried as her eldest son's name was called and he walked across the stage in his maroon cap and gown.

The city of Compton, on the southern periphery of Los Angeles, was proud that they had elected a Negro Mayor and City Council as the largest Negro run city in California. They tried hard to encourage businesses to move into their community. They struggled to control the underlying problems of poverty and too many single parent households. Latch-key children, alone too many hours, found easy friendships in gangs where guns and drive-by shootings measured a teen's maturity and pregnancies were too common. Patrick Chavis had survived. He had beaten the odds and successfully completed the first leg of his education.

Confident and smiling, and with letters of recommendation from his Minister, Patrick applied and was accepted into Albion, a small Liberal Arts College that had been founded a hundred years earlier by the Methodist Church. It was set in a small Michigan town, two hundred miles west of Detroit. The nervous teen said a tearful goodbye to his mother, sisters and brother, as he boarded the train at Los Angeles' Union Station for the three day trip. It would be his first time away from home, and his family, but he was ready...frightened a little, but ready.

Patrick was a good student but the work was difficult. His high school work hadn't really prepared him for the rigor of a college curriculum. Friends and teachers helped and he made passing grades. As he had promised his mother, he wrote home weekly. He came home for the summer and worked whenever he could find a job. When fall rolled around, he'd get back on the train and return to Albion. Four years later, Patrick Chavis graduated with a degree in Biology. His hairline had receded and he now needed glasses but he had risen above his beginnings and he was filled with ambition. He wasn't through with his education, however. Now he wanted to get into Medical School.

America had struggled with a variety of programs for more than a hundred years to right the wrongs of slavery. What was the best way to provide an opportunity...a doorway, to upward mobility for those who had been economically, educationally, and socially disadvantaged? *'Separate but equal'* had only been abolished by the Supreme Court in their 1954 decision in Brown v. The Board of Education of Topeka. Was it acceptable to consider the issue of race in housing, education, and hiring?

There had always been restrictions on acceptance to medical schools, more students applying than openings available. Limits on the number of women or Jews that would be accepted existed well into the 20th century. Now the issue of less academically qualified Negroes was the issue...social equality or the best medical graduates. The scales tipped to and fro.

Patrick Chavis was accepted to the University of California – Davis Medical School where they had set aside sixteen slots out of one hundred to accept minority students and add to the diversity of their program.

Those sixteen slots meant that Allan Bakke, having successfully graduated from the University of California – Berkeley, and received his Bachelor's degree, was denied acceptance. He was angry and frustrated. He had given up a portion of his life to serve his country and those lost years were now preventing him from pursuing the career he wanted so desperately. He filed suit alleging that the University of California – Davis' special admissions program operated to exclude him on the basis of his race in violation of the Equal Protection Clause of the Fourteenth Amendment. A substantial portion of Allan Bakke's argument focused on the results of the Medical College Admissions Test. They revealed how much more qualified he was than applicants who had been accepted because of their race:

The following chart shows the MCAT scores for the rejected white medical school applicant, Allan Bakke, in 1973 vs. other "diversity" admissions:

	College GPA	MCAT verbal score	MCAT quantitative score	MCAT science score	MCAT general information score
Allan Bakke's 1973 scores:	3.46	96th percentile	94th percentile	97th percentile	72nd percentile
Average "diversity" student's scores:	2.88	46th percentile	24th percentile	35th percentile	33rd percentile

A similar issue of reverse discrimination was occurring in the Midwest.

"Sweetheart," Barbara Grutter said, as she poured coffee for her husband at their small home in Plymouth, Michigan. "How do you feel about me going back to college? I want to become a health-care attorney." The mother of two young sons and manager of a small information technology business, blonde, white, and attractive, she was restless.

"I had a strong grade point average when I received my undergraduate degree and I she still have that fire within me. I want to accomplish more."

"That was eighteen years ago, Barbara, but the kids and I will suck it up if that's what you want," her husband responded. "But only if I get another cup of coffee before I leave for work."

She was surprised and disappointed when she was denied admission to the University of Michigan's Law School. But it was reading an article in the Detroit Free Press a few weeks later that really upset her. That story detailed how lower performing minority students were being accepted into Universities around the state. She didn't hesitate. She contacted the Center for Individual Rights, a pro bono organization eager to prosecute such affirmative action cases, and agreed to become the Plaintiff in a law suit against the University, contending that less qualified students, always minorities, had been accepted, taken the limited number of spaces available, and unfairly disadvantaged her. Her suit, Grutter vs. Bollinger, head of the University of Michigan's Admissions, would move forward.

Both suits, Bakke vs. the Regents of the University of California and Grutter vs. Bollinger would eventually make their slow plodding way to the U.S. Supreme Court. The decisions would be a quarter century apart, 1978 and 2003, and both would be resolved by 5-4 decisions. Only one Justice, William Rehnquist, would hear both cases.

The 1970s, in which these events played themselves out, was a period of accelerated social unrest. The 1960's had seen Martin Luther King and the Civil Rights movement make the country conscious of racial disparities...marches, strikes and 'blowback' by southern whites were beginning to shake the social fabric of the country. The atrocities and losses of life from the Vietnam War had made many Americans distrustful of their government. We were not been an equal opportunity country. Black, Latino, and Women's movements enlisted tens of thousands to make their voices heard. Historical bastions of male white supremacy were under attack and when the pendulum of equality overreached, there was a backlash.

Allan Bakke's lawsuit was such a backlash. He was white, male, a veteran, and qualified. His suit against the University was filed in 1974. He had been rejected twice by UC-Davis' Admissions committee, citing that *"economically and/or educationally disadvantaged"* minority applicants would get special consideration. The University defended its enrollment process at the Medical School, contending that its goal was to reduce the historic deficit of minorities in medical schools and the medical profession, counter the effects of discrimination in society, increase the number of physicians who would likely practice in underserved communities, and obtain the educational benefits that flow from an ethnically diverse student body. In responding to Mr. Bakke's rejection, the University's Special Admissions Committee stated they would consider only candidates who were from explicitly designated minority groups.

The lower court found that the special program operated as a racial quota. Minority applicants in that program were rated only against one another and not against all students who had applied. The Medical School could not satisfy its burden of demonstrating that, absent the special program, Bakke would not have been admitted, the court ordered his admission to the Medical School. The decision was appealed to a higher court.

When the case of *Regents of the University of California v. Bakke* reached the Supreme Court in October 1977 Jimmy Carter was President, New York City had endured a twenty-five hour blackout, and the television miniseries, Roots, had captivated the nation.

Warren Burger was Chief Justice. The court's Associate justices were William Brennan, Potter Stewart, Byron White, Thurgood Marshall, Harry Blackmun, Lewis Powell, William Rehnquist and John Stevens. Nine elderly men, one of them Negro, and no women, would decide the case. Several of the Justices tenure dated back to the activist court of Earl Warren but it now lacked a charismatic leader.

Title VI of the 1964 Civil Rights Act was clear: *No person in the United States shall, on the ground of race, color, or national origin, be excluded from participation in, be denied the benefits of, or be subjected to discrimination under any program or activity receiving Federal financial assistance.*

But this wasn't a minority being denied admission...this was a qualified white male being denied admission. Did Title VI apply? That certainly was never the intent. The members of the court struggled with how to approach the Bakke case.

Was it a statutory or Constitutional question? Did it violate the Civil Rights Act or did it violate the Fourteenth Amendment guaranteeing equal rights to all? If it was reverse discrimination, is the court required to measure the degree of that discrimination and what standards should be applied? Even the Justices were vexed as to what legal right should take precedence.

Three justices concurred that the UC-Davis admissions policy used race in a benign way as part of an affirmative action program and had never been intended to use race as an exclusionary qualification.

"Please circulate memoranda on your thoughts before we try and have a definitive conference vote," Burger urged, aware of the confusing issues this case presented. For the next four months memos flowed between the offices of the Justices. Each was turned over to one of the Justice's clerks to research and comment on.

Chilly autumn weather was blowing through Washington D.C. Thanksgiving was just weeks away and still the court had not reached a consensus, vexed by the contradictory issues and trying to remain apart from the winds of opinion shouted from newspapers and placards outside the court.

"While circulating memos is not our usual practice," Justice Rehnquist wrote, "I have derived some benefit from reading Justice Whites' and those written by other brethren's subsequent written communications. I also think that some written comments on a case this complicated and multifaceted could save a lot of time in what is bound to be a long Conference discussion anyway."

Chief Justice Burger's memo was more outspoken. The Court must find a way 'to affirm the California Supreme Court without putting the states, their universities, or any educational institution in a straitjacket on the matter of broader based admission programs. We cannot be in the business of establishing fixed ground rules for educators. The Davis program, as presently structured is one of the more extreme methods of securing commendable objectives.'

Rehnquist, a noted strict constructionist had decided that Davis' affirmative action policy was difficult to support based on the Fourteenth Amendment. "I take it as a postulate," he said, "That difference in the treatment of individuals based on their race or ethnic origin is at the bulls-eye of the target at which the Fourteenth Amendment Equal Protection clause was aimed."

The liberal members of the court, Justices White, Marshall, and Brennan were determined to support the university's admission program. They believed it was a legitimate and sincere effort to address the consequences of centuries of discrimination against Negroes and other minorities. How they could achieve this without destroying the 14th Amendment had not been worked out.

Justice Thurgood Marshall, the court's only African-American, and a man who had fought the sting of discrimination as chief legal counsel for the NAACP, was more adamant.

"The decision in this case depends on whether you consider the actions of the Regents of the university as admitting certain students or as excluding certain other students. Several of our brethren view their program as an attempt to remove the last vestiges of slavery and state imposed segregation. If you view their program as excluding students, it is a program of quotas which violates the principle that our Constitution is color-blind...take your choice."

Justice Thurgood Marshall

Then he added, with a clear sarcasm, "As to this country being a melting pot, either the Negro did not get into the pot or he did not get melted down. If only the principle of color-blindness had been accepted by the majority in Plessy (*v. Ferguson, 1896, deciding that separate but equal was acceptable and states could adapt their own policies, the 14th Amendment only applied to Federal issues*), we would not be facing this problem in 1978. For us now to say that the principle of color-blindness prevents the University from giving special consideration to race when this same Court in 1896 licensed the states to continue to consider race, is to make a mockery of the principle of equal justice under the law."

Harry Blackmun had been absent from the court for several months during these considerations, recovering from prostate cancer and, with no unanimity of opinion, Justice Burger delayed finalizing a vote. He was eager to have the entire court weigh in on this case. Meanwhile, the other eight judges agreed on some issues, disagreed on others.

So far four Justices had concurred that simply using race as one criterion was not in and of itself unconstitutional, but they could reach no agreement on what standards to use or how race was to be used. It took until early May for Justice Blackmun to be well enough to join in and to read the copious material that each justice had written and make his decision. He concurred with the positions of Justices Marshall, Brennan, White, and Powell that including race as one criterion was acceptable. He rebutted Rehnquist's rigid, color-blind thinking. "We do not live in an ideal world," he said. "We live in a real world. Title VI and the Fourteenth Amendment deal with the unconstitutional use of race criteria, not with the use of race as an appropriate remedy feature."

It was the end of June 1978 when the nine justices of the United States Supreme Court were able to consolidate their independent conclusions. Their opinion continued to be divided as to whether the Davis admissions program exceeded good judgment and the justices would concur or dissent on sections of the majority opinion. In the end, however, affirmative action programs were acknowledged as necessary efforts as long as they were not the only considerations. The court, in a 5-4 vote, accepted the principle of affirmative action, recognizing the America's obligations to its minorities. By one vote the nation's acknowledgment of the need for social justice had prevailed.

The court ordered Allan Bakke's admission. He began his studies at the University of California Medical School at Davis in the fall of 1978. Bakke graduated in 1982, and completed his residency as an intern at the famed Mayo Clinic in Rochester, Minnesota.

Meanwhile Patrick Chavis had entered Medical School at the University of California at Davis in 1973 under their minority, i.e. special admissions, program. He graduated and began his practice just as Allan Bakke walked the corridors of the same campus.

After he graduated, Dr. Chavis opened his practice as an OB/GYN in Southwest Los Angeles, a predominantly Negro and Latino enclave. He married and had a family. He was hailed nationally as a successful example of affirmative action...a poster child for equal opportunity. But a strange turn of events awaited him.

A new procedure, Liposuction, was becoming popular, and lucrative. There was no shortage of women in Southern California who yearned to have a slimmer waist line. Dr. Chavis signed up to attend an intense four day seminar at the Liposuction Institute of Beverly Hills but after two days he left, convinced he had grasped the essentials. He immediately changed his practice to the 'New Attitude Body Sculpting Clinic,' offering liposuction to his patients.

Within months, however, Dr. Chavis inexplicitly began to change. His attitude became callous. A year after opening up his new practice, his first medical disaster occurred. Yolanda Mukhalian lost 70% of her blood during her liposuction procedure and rather than being taken to the hospital, Dr. Chavis stashed her at his home for several days. She barely survived. A year later Valerie Lawrence was brought in by her sister and following her procedure, the doctor, once again, took her to his home, the IV still connected, the patient still bleeding. Had Ms. Lawrence's sister not insisted on getting her to the hospital, she might have died. Then disaster struck. In June 1996 a young married woman came to him, not sick, just wanting to look better. Tammaria Cotton kissed her husband and left him sitting in the waiting room.

"I'll be back within two hours and I'll be beautiful," she said. "You won't even recognize me."

In the middle of the procedure Tammaria began bleeding profusely. Dr. Chavis sent her home with her husband; the bleeding had been stemmed but not stopped. Mr. Cotton barely got her to a hospital before she died of cardiac arrest. There were just too many complaints and in 1997 the California Medical Board suspended Patrick Chavis' license to practice. It was permanently revoked in 1998. At that point he had been sued 21 times in a 21 year career. A life that looked so promising had fallen apart.

On a quiet summer evening in 2002, Dr. Chavis stopped at a neighborhood Foster's Freeze to get an ice cream. Three unknown teens hijacked his car and shot him. Those who had once heaped praise on him and the righteousness of racial quotas now faced the outcries of those who had condemned such programs.

*****

Meanwhile Barbara Grutter's case moved tortuously through the lower courts. Her legal costs continued to be paid for by the Center for Individual Rights, a non-profit public interest law firm based in Washington, D.C. The Center believed itself to be nonpartisan but it was clearly conservative and libertarian in its positions. The group's primary focus was the enforcement of constitutional limits on state and federal power, primarily through litigation. Most of what it regards as unconstitutional, or unlawful preference, revolves around issues of race, sex, or some other protected status. Barbara Grutter's reverse discrimination case was a perfect cause for them. She had been excluded from a University that chose to favor minorities over nonminorities…it was an affirmative action issue, similar to that of the Bakke case. The Center wanted Justice Lewis Powell's majority opinion in that case declared legally wrong. That opinion, which had endorsed diversity as a reason for states to engage in racial preferences in university admissions, represented everything to which they were opposed.

The U.S. District Court had found that the University of Michigan Law School's use of race as an acceptance criterion to be excessive. The case then moved up to the Circuit Court which reversed the District Court's decision, citing the Bakke's case as precedent. The Supreme Court agreed to hear the case.

Justice Sandra Day O'Connor, once again in a 5-4 decision, wrote the majority opinion. It held that the United States Constitution *"does not prohibit the law school's narrowly tailored use of race in admissions decisions to further a compelling interest in obtaining the educational benefits that flow from a diverse student body."* The Court held that the law school's interest in obtaining a *"critical mass"* of minority students was indeed a *"tailored use."* She noted, in an unusually personal note that sometime in the future, racial affirmative action would no longer be necessary in order to promote diversity. *"Affirmative action should not be allowed permanent status and that eventually a 'colorblind' policy should be implemented. Race-conscious admissions policies must be limited in time."*

Barbara Grutter lost her case and the admission policies of the University of Michigan were upheld. But in an unpredictable twist another case, decided around the same time, yielded an entirely different result. Jennifer Gratz and Patrick Hamacher, both white Michigan residents, applied for admission to the University of Michigan's undergraduate College of Literature, Science, and the Arts (LSA). They were denied admission two years apart but for the same reasons.

Justice Sandra Day O'Conner

The University of Michigan had used a 150-point scale to rank freshman applicants with 100 points needed to guarantee admission. The University gave underrepresented ethnic groups, including African-Americans, Hispanics, and Native Americans, an automatic 20-point bonus on this scale, while a perfect SAT score was worth only 12 points. Under this point system, neither Ms. Gratz nor Mr. Hamacher was accepted. A few years later their case was heard by the Supreme Court. And by a 6-3 decision, Justice Rehnquist decided that these policies were too overreaching and mechanistic in its use of race as a factor in admissions, and were, therefore, unconstitutional.

In the decades since these cases Universities have become more cautious in their use of race as a criterion, but there is no doubt that despite its failures, affirmative action programs have provided opportunities for minority students that would not have otherwise existed.

In 1978, Justice Lewis Powell, in writing a majority 5-4 decision in the Allan Bakke case and nearly twenty years later, Justice Sandra Day O'Conner, writing the majority 5-4 decision in the Barbara Grutter case, confirmed the use of racial quotas as a consideration for college admissions. By single votes, the country had reaffirmed its desire to ameliorate the evils of slavery.

IX

ABORTION & THE SUPREME COURT

The church bells rang from the nearby Baptist Church competing with those tolling from a Methodist Church a mile away. It was a late spring Sunday morning on the last day of May, 2009, and the good people of Omaha, Nebraska were being beckoned to enter their house of God and cleanse their sins. Overcoats had been stored away in the basement closet. With luck, the weather would be hospitable, there would be enough rain for a good crop, and their galoshes, snow tires, and mufflers wouldn't be needed again for several months. Dr. Leroy Carhart, a retired Air Force officer, was at his clinic on the outskirts of the city when his cell phone began to vibrate. It wasn't unusual for the doctor to be working on a Sunday …he had a very controversial practice. It was a little after ten in the morning, and he was already scrubbed and in surgery. Sunday was often a busy day for protesters in front of his clinic, but for some unknown reason, there were no pickets or signs today to harass the women, who had come, already nervous, having taken another step toward their decision. The clinic was light and airy, doing what it could to dispel the women's unsettled emotions.

The doctor ignored the telephone interruption and finished the procedure before looking to see who had called. The caller ID indicated that it had come from a friend and cohort, George Tiller, head practitioner at a similar facility short hours away in Wichita, Kansas. The timing was unusual; the two men rarely needed to speak to one another Sunday mornings. Thinking it might be an emergency …something related to a patient, Dr. Carhart returned the call. The telephone at the other end rang several times before a familiar voice answered. It was Dr. Tiller's nurse and she was sobbing incoherently. "George is dead," she told him through sobs, relaying the news that George Tiller, a wonderful man he'd had the pleasure of working with for the past several years, had been fatally shot attending Sunday services at his Lutheran church.

These two men shared the dangerous occupation of performing late-term, also known as partial-birth, abortions. A late-term abortion is one in which an induced abortion procedure is performed after the 20th week of gestation. However, the exact date on which a pregnancy becomes late-term is not clearly defined. Some sources define any abortion after sixteen weeks as late-term. Most abortions, conducted so late in the pregnancy, involve the partial birth procedure of intact dilation and fetal extraction. It is a far less frequent, but far more controversial, procedure and the doctors who perform them are the target of militant right-to-life groups around the country. George Tiller had been murdered in front of his family by one of their more extreme followers.

Dr. Carhart had been scheduled to work in Dr. Tiller's clinic the next day. He was one of three doctors who took turns at the clinic and were willing to perform abortions, both traditional as well as late-term. His car was already packed for the five-hour drive from Omaha to Wichita, the same drive he made every third Sunday for the past five years. His hands were shaking and his eyes red as he realized the impact of what had happened. He decided he would still make the trip, see Tiller's family, and help figure out what would happen to the clinic.

Dr. Leroy Carhart

He closed the door to his small office and buried his head in his hands. He wanted to shut out the world. He wanted to blank out all the insanity and violence. He, Tiller, and their associates believed in what they were doing. They were helping women and married couples who most often had few options. There were reasons why he and the other doctors did what they did. It had all changed for him in 1987, when a nurse prevailed on him to spend a day at the abortion clinic where she worked. Talking to the women reminded him of the patients he had seen as a medical student, prior to the Supreme Court's ground-breaking decision, in the famous case of Roe v. Wade. They confirmed that the right to an abortion fell within a woman's right to privacy. No longer did there need to be dark days when women were forced to use coat hangers or seek some incompetent quack, functioning out of a back room...women whose botched abortions left them with perforated uteruses, intestines protruding from the vagina, or untreatable pelvic infections. The way Carhart remembered, before that decision it was a good week for the emergency room if only five women died after arriving with the effects of botched abortions.

He shook himself back to reality. He had patients who needed him. He would have to deal with his grief later. His waiting room, after all, was full of women who'd crossed state lines and waited hours to see him. He put on new scrubs, sterilized his hands, and returned to the operating room to perform another abortion and visit his post-op patients.

"Hi Cynthia, how are you feeling?" Carhart said as he stopped at the bedside of a woman he'd worked on earlier in the day. She was crying.

"I'm fine Dr. Carhart. I'm just not sure I did the right thing. Was it a boy or a girl," she said, her eyes damp, her forehead furrowed. Her damp, mousy brown hair clung to her face. She had driven in from Lincoln yesterday, sixteen weeks pregnant, having left her two younger children at home with her boyfriend.

"It was a boy and I can't tell you whether you did the right thing. What you did was make a difficult decision."

"I didn't know I was pregnant until last week and I know my boyfriend would walk out if he found out I was pregnant again. Usually he wears a condom, but not always," she confessed.

"Well, you rest. Another hour or two and you can head home," he smiled and moved down the corridor. Before most of Omaha's families sat down to their Sunday dinner, Dr. Carhart had helped another dozen women.

*****

George Tiller, a relaxed, bespectacled man, who loved his family and the work he did, had been serving as an usher during morning services at the Reformation Lutheran

Dr. George Tiller

Church where he and his wife and children attended most Sundays. It was ten in the morning. Their one son was away at college, hoping to be a doctor and follow in his father's footsteps. Jeanne, his wife, was in the choir, wearing their burgundy robes and chatting with other choristers when shots rang out and the sound ricocheted across the church. She and the other choir members could only watch, stunned and helpless, as the entire horrifying events unfolded mere yards away. The killer, a 51 year old bald, sallow complexioned man, Scott Roeder, approached Dr. Tiller and fired point blank into his face. Tiller had been wearing body armor these past years on the recommendation of the FBI. He had already been attacked on multiple occasions by other crazed militants, but standing only three feet from a man intent on killing him, his body armor was worthless. Dr. Tiller had only seconds to react as his eyes connected with the dark expressionless eyes of the man across from him. Roeder didn't speak. He lifted the hand gun from his side, pointed and fired. Several witnesses to the shooting attempted to intervene and chase the gunman down, but he was able to flee in his blue Ford Taurus. Several hours later, the Police apprehended him near Gardner, three hours from Kansas City. He was quickly identified as having been associated with Operation Rescue.

Operation Rescue, the nation's largest right-to-life organization, had been vilifying Dr. Tiller, Dr. Carhart, and other doctors and clinics that performed abortions for more than a decade. Tiller and Carhart had been among the few U.S. physicians performing late-term abortion, making them a favored target of anti-abortion protesters. Tiller testified that he and his family had suffered years of harassment and threats. His clinic was bombed in 1985, and it became the primary target of the 1991 *"Summer of Mercy"* protests marked by mass demonstrations and arrests.   Thousands arrived in Wichita that summer, led by Keith Tucci, National Director of Operation Rescue.   They blocked streets and conducted sit-ins at the three medical clinics that performed abortions.   They shouted epithets and obscenities as young and middle-age women tried to enter.   Over sixteen hundred arrests took place during the first three weeks, with thousands of locals gathering and dozens of clergy people becoming involved.

"They're in there killing babies, nothing else, ma'am," John Snow, an elderly retired accountant told a newspaper reporter as he handed her a glass of Kool-Aid.

Pastor Keith and Penny Tucci

The crowd departed in early August, ending with a prayer gathering that filled the thirty thousand seat Cessna Stadium. By the events end, six weeks later, the Wichita Police had made over twenty-six hundred arrests.

When the Supreme Court released its decision on *Roe v. Wade*, most American evangelicals were not politically active. By the 1980's, however, thanks to people like Keith Tucci and Phyllis Schlafly, national spokeswoman against the Equal Rights Amendment, the question of abortion became a litmus test for political office or appointment to a Federal Court.

Schlafly called *Roe v. Wade* "the worst decision in the history of the U.S. Supreme Court.

"It is responsible for the killing of millions of unborn babies," she thundered in meeting after meeting. The pro-life movement had been galvanized, and, made euphoric by the election of two pro-life presidents, both named Bush. The furor and controversy sparked by the nonviolent prayer rescues and the blocking of abortion clinics received coverage in the national media and, although negative, it ensured that the Operation Rescue movement was not going to die quietly.

The issue of when a fetus becomes a human being is the milieu of religion and the individual beliefs within a society, neither of which had kept pace with medical advances that permitted many more third trimester infants to survive. Did the ultimate decision rest with the mother who carried the baby, or society? Should the decision involve the medical condition of the mother or infant...should the decision include factors such as the mother's ability to raise the child, the presence of a father, the age of the mother, or whether the pregnancy arose from consensual sex or rape?

While the country argued these issues, George Tiller continued to be a target. An abortion opponent shot him in both arms in 1993.   Operation Rescue maintained a "Tiller Watch" feature on its website, but, at least publicly, they were quick to condemn the shooting.

Dr. Carhart was still in Wichita, overseeing Dr. Tiller's clinic and comforting the family when his daughter, still back in Omaha, received a late-night phone call saying her parents, too, had been killed.   The caller laughed as he made the gruesome statement.   The next day his clinic got suspicious letters containing white powder.   Murder would not satisfy their lust.

"We are shocked at this morning's disturbing news that Mr. Tiller was gunned down. Operation Rescue has worked for years through peaceful, legal means, and through the proper channels to see him brought to justice. We denounce vigilantism and the cowardly act that took place this morning. We pray for Mr. Tiller's family that they will find comfort and healing that can only be found in Jesus Christ."

"Preborn children's lives were in imminent danger," Roeder shouted as he was pushed, handcuffed, into the court house.

This wasn't Scott Roeder's first encounter with the legal system.   He had been arrested as an anti-government protester. Police officers searching his car discovered explosives charges, a fuse cord, gunpowder, and nine-volt batteries in the trunk.   Roeder freely admitted that he knew David Leach, publisher of *Prayer & Action News*, a magazine that openly supports the killing of abortion providers as justifiable homicide.

Leach was also the publisher of the Army of God manual, which advocates the killing of the providers of abortion and contains bomb-making instructions. Despite Roeder's defense team trying to claim their client's mental instability, he was found guilty of first-degree murder and sentenced to life imprisonment without parole.

Scott Roeder

His imprisonment did not dissolve the rancor that surrounded the subject. In 1991 the state of Nebraska passed a law mandating parental notification. It required teens to get a signed statement from their parents authorizing their daughter to have a procedure that could terminate her pregnancy or, if that wasn't practical, to get a court order.

By 1991 and the passage of the law, Dr. Carhart had been performing abortions for nearly a decade. Two days after the law was passed the Doctor's farm was burned down, killing a large number of his horses and family pets. It had been started simultaneously in seven separate locations.

The fire inspectors were never able to determine the fire's cause or arrest those who had started it, but Dr. Carhart knew.   The next day his clinic received a letter justifying the murder of abortion providers. The sidewalks leading to his clinic have been smeared with manure. Protesters stalked him in airports. In the face of all this intimidation his clinic refused to back down.   His clinic's sign, *ABORTION & CONTRACEPTION CLINIC OF NEBRASKA*, proclaimed his bravery in four foot high letters.

*****

Until the Roe v. Wade decision in 1973, abortion laws were controlled by the separate states.   Then, the rules changed. Abortion had now been legalized at the Federal level and state laws that conflicted with it had been made invalid overnight.   The case arose when a young, pregnant woman wanted to obtain a safe and legal abortion.   To protect her identity, she was given the name 'Jane Roe,' and filed a suit to overthrow an 1859 Texas law banning abortion. The case finally made its way to the Supreme Court which determined that the right to privacy gave women the right to obtain an abortion legally at any point during the first months of pregnancy. The decision reached in *Roe v. Wade* allowed women to obtain abortions regardless of location or social status. It invalidated all state abortion laws, except those that allowed abortion to protect the lives of women.   It reduced the shame and dangers of terminating an unwanted pregnancy that had existed. But the high court's decision in

Roe v. Wade didn't quell the arguments about abortion, it only intensified them.

The Supreme Court had set the rules on providing comprehensive protection of elective abortions. But the farther along a pregnancy gets, and with each biological milestone a fetus passes, survival rates increase and Americans become more cautious and conflicted in their attitudes. Sometime around the twenty-fourth week of pregnancy, when the fetus has a better chance of surviving outside the womb, the right to terminate becomes most controversial, and abortion least accessible. *Roe* recognized the unique status of late-term abortions and gave states the power to restrict or disallow abortion when the fetus is viable, with an exception for 'the preservation of the life or health of the mother.'

Birth rates in the United States have leveled out at fewer than four million a year. Total annual abortions have leveled at about 1.2 million, but the rate for Negro and Latina women is more than three times that for Caucasian women. All rates have dropped since non-medical procedures, such as Mifepristone, RU-486, also called *'the morning after'* drug, became available. A much higher percent of medically-induced abortions now deal with *"viability."* No rational doctor will terminate a pregnancy without a compelling reason. But what is a compelling reason, and who decides? Is a fetal abnormality, mental or physical, a compelling reason?

What percentage chance of surviving outside the womb is acceptable? Doctors who perform abortions deal with such decisions constantly. They must also deal with an infinite array of emotions facing a pregnant woman conflicted over how she wants to proceed.

The day after Dr. Tiller's funeral, Dr. Carhart visited a patient, an attractive co-ed, about the same age as Dr. Tiller's son. Sarah Kingsley, a sophomore at the University of Kansas, had been the victim of a brutal campus rape one night as she was returning to her dorm after an evening in the library. She was now in the third trimester of her pregnancy. Why didn't she get an abortion sooner? Bearing the rapist's child was tormenting her but getting an abortion was against her religious beliefs.

"Every time I feel the baby move, it brings back the rape all over again," Sarah had told the admitting nurse. She tried counseling several times, but the horror of that night remained with her. She'd made three unsuccessful suicide attempts.

"If a woman is going to kill herself, then I think you have to look at the option of an abortion for both her mental and physical health," Carhart said before he agreed to do the procedure.

The political activism of the right-to-life movement had begun influencing legislation. Operation Rescue and The National Right to Life Committee helped define the exact words included in Nebraska's Partial Birth Abortion Law:

An abortion in which the person performing the abortion, deliberately and intentionally vaginally delivers a living fetus until, in the case of a head-first presentation, the entire fetal head is outside the body of the mother, or, in the case of breech presentation, any part of the fetal trunk past the navel is outside the body of the mother, for the purpose of performing an overt act that the person knows will kill the partially delivered living fetus; and performs the overt act, other than completion of delivery, that kills the partially delivered living fetus.

Dr. Carhart decided to challenge the law and filed a suit against the Nebraska Attorney General, Donald Stenberg. The case of *Stenberg v. Carhart* reached the Supreme Court in 2000. It was Dr. Carhart's goal to overturn the Nebraska law which made performing partial-birth abortions illegal, except where necessary to save the life of the mother. Nebraska physicians who performed the procedure contrary to the law were subject to having their medical licenses revoked. Dr. Carhart and his supporters were convinced the only basis for the law was a unilaterally ill-defined 'public morality.'

In 2000 the Supreme Court continued to be divided philosophically between liberal and conservative factions. William Rehnquist, now Chief Justice, was supported by Justices Clarence Thomas and Antonin Scalia in forming a solid conservative bloc. They were often joined in their decisions by Justice Anthony Kennedy. The more liberal justices included Justices Steven Breyer, John Paul Stevens, Ruth Bader Ginsburg, and David Souter. On most issues the remaining Justice, Sandra Day O'Conner, voted with her Conservative brethren. But justices are human, and being a woman, she recognized the sensitivity of the issues before the court. She voted with Justice Ginsburg, the Court's other female justice, and the liberal faction to strike down the law. By her one vote, she succeeded in protecting the rights of women to make their own decision on a complicated emotional issue.

"Any abortion law that imposes an undue burden on a woman's 'right to choose' is unconstitutional. Causing those who procure abortions to 'fear prosecution, conviction, and imprisonment' is an undue burden, and, therefore, I declare the law to be against the Constitution," averred Justice Stephen Breyer, in writing the Court's majority opinion. Dr. Carhart had won this round.

*****

A few years later, however, George Bush edged out Al Gore for the Presidency and there was a new Republican administration in Washington, and a new U.S. Attorney General, Alberto Gonzalez. Two years earlier President Bill Clinton, Democrat, shared power with a Republican legislature. The Congress had passed a Federal law prohibiting Partial Birth abortions but Clinton vetoed it and the Congress was unable to amass enough votes to override his veto.

But now 'there was a new Sheriff in town.' Two other significant changes had also taken place since the Stenberg v.

Carhart decision. The makeup of the Court that had validated Dr. Carhart's position had changed. Chief Justice William Rehnquist had retired and been replaced by John Roberts, who shared a comparable conservative ideology. Sandra Day O'Conner, ill, had held off her retirement until the 2000 Presidential election returned the Republicans to the White House. She was replaced by Samuel Alito, an ultra-conservative jurist.

The Partial Birth Abortion Ban Act that had been vetoed by Bill Clinton had been resubmitted, passed, and signed by the new President, George Bush. Under this law "Any physician who, in or affecting interstate or foreign commerce, knowingly performs a partial-birth abortion and thereby kills a human fetus shall be fined under this title or imprisoned not more than 2 years, or both." *Roe v. Wade* had been narrowed, and Dr. Carhart, and others like him, were now the target of both 'right to life' advocates and the Federal government.

The new law was in conflict with the high court's previous ruling in Stenberg v. Carhart and Alberto Gonzalez set out to rectify the matter armed with new ammunition. He filed a new suit in District Court, Gonzalez v. Carhart, and by 2007 the case had reached the Supreme Court...a newly configured Court. The decision was once again 5-4 but this time, without Sandra Day O'Conner, the conservative jurists prevailed. Dr. Carhart's ability to perform late term abortions had been made illegal and how many women would be affected by the change from Justice O'Conner to

Justice Alito will never be known, once again one vote was changing the direction of society.

At today's level of medical knowledge, many studies show a fetus's chance of survival to be above fifty percent at twenty-four weeks. Survival rates before then drop rapidly...at twenty-two weeks it's less than ten percent. But such clear guidelines are not always present. Each case needs to be evaluated independently without strict laws that inhibit qualified medical decisions. Since Dr. Tiller's murder, there are less than ten doctors nationwide willing to perform such late-term procedures. Dr. Leroy Carhart is one of them and the country remains divided on the question of what is the moral solution.

X

PATRIOTISM & THE AMERICAN FLAG

The words of Francis Scott Key have long echoed in the soul of Americans... *"The rocket's red glare, the bombs bursting in air, gave proof through the night that our flag was still there."* From the stories of Betsy Ross and the thirteen colonies, the stars and stripes have come to define the independent and proud character of our country. As children, we learned the Pledge of Allegiance *'to the flag of the United States of America...'* It is one of our nation's most enduring symbols and anyone who dares to trample on our flag tramples on everything that America holds sacred. But is it logical to place such power in a piece of cloth. Is it a talisman? Does it somehow hold magical powers? Would our country be threatened ideologically or morally if our flag was damaged? Would the battle really be lost if the soldier carrying the flag into conflict was killed? Did the planting of the flag on Iwo Jima define the battle, or American pride? The Civil War evoked strong emotions surrounding the importance of the flag as a symbol of belief. Union troops carried the Stars & Stripes proudly into battle. And, even after the war ended, the Southern states continued to fly their Confederate Flag in defiance. For the following century that flag adorned court houses and schools...a symbol of continued white superiority.

As the twentieth century began, businesses began a flagrant use of the stars and stripes in the advertising of products ranging from magical elixirs to bawdy shows. States began to pass a variety of laws to prevent desecration of this national symbol, including specifications as to how the flag was to be flown or positioned in relation to state flags.

It wasn't until 1907 that the United States Supreme Court sought to define a national policy regarding this national symbol. What was legal in one state was illegal in another and it had become impossible for businesses operating in all states to establish consistent policies. Desecration, marking, or otherwise defacing a flag design, using the flag in commercial advertising, and showing "contempt" for the flag in any way--by public burning it, trampling on it, spitting on it, or otherwise showing a lack of respect for it was defined differently in the north than it was out west, different in the southern states than in the New England states.

In 1903, the State of Nebraska passed a law making it a crime to 'sell, expose for sale, or have in possession for sale, any article of merchandise upon which shall have been printed or placed, for purposes of advertisement, a representation of the flag of the United States.' A year later George Halter, owner of a local bottling company was charged with selling a bottle of beer with a prominent American flag on its label for the purpose of advertisement. Halter argued that the law violated his freedom of speech and the principle of federalism.

"The American flag," he said, "Is designated by the national government and represents the whole of America;

therefore, the authority to regulate the use of the flag lies with the federal government rather than with the states."

The case reached the Supreme Court and Justice John Harlan, writing for an 8-1 majority wrote:

> *For that flag every true American has not simply an appreciation, but a deep affection. No American, nor any foreign-born person who enjoys the privileges of American citizenship, ever looks upon it without taking pride in the fact that he lives under this free government. One who loves the Union will love the state in which he resides, and love both of the common country and of the state will diminish in proportion as respect for the flag is weakened. Therefore a state ... will be impatient if any open disrespect is shown towards it. ... It is familiar law that even the privileges of citizenship and the rights inhering in personal liberty are subject ... to such reasonable restraints as may be required for the general good.*

American pride and the flag had morphed into one and that attitude would dominate through the travails of World War I, be tested by a decade of economic trauma, and be resurrected for World War II. Presidents, military leaders, and office seekers would cloak themselves in the flag...this was America and our flag meant freedom, opportunity, and a unique way of life. In sports venues, parades, and holidays we raised our flag high.

Justice John Harlan

But the patriotism of World War II was weakened and questioned as the undeclared Korean War lacked the moral persuasion that had always been so clear when American soldiers were dying in combat. A new, younger, generation began to question their parent's dictum of *'my country, right or wrong, my country!'* And, before the guns had cooled from battles at Pusan and the Yalu River, and the bodies of brave young men were being buried at the Arlington National Cemetery, we began sending military advisors into someplace called French Indo-China …Vietnam.

Fear of the spread of Communism traumatized our government. We saw the enemy everywhere. The righteousness of Western civilization depended on American military might and resolve. Arnold Toynbee, a British historian, championed his *'domino theory.'* One by one, he said, the country's of Southeast Asia would fall like dominos and be brought under control of the evil empire of Communist China. It had little historic validity but when the French were ousted from their colony, the United States became convinced of their need to support the southern Vietnamese people fighting the Chinese-supported north and its leader, Ho Chi Minh.

Three Presidents, more than fifty thousand American dead, in addition to nearly a million north Vietnamese killed, and the war was no closer to resolution...the Tet offensive...the bombing of Haiphong Harbor...repeated lies and omissions of the war's progress and the shooting of four students at a Kent State University protest led to an increasing vocal war protest movement. The 1968 Democratic convention was the scene of violence and reaction. Patriotism and the flag were no longer sacrosanct. At an event in New York's Central Park, peace activists burned American flags in protest against the Vietnam War. In response, Congress passed the Federal Flag Desecration Law. The law banned any display of "contempt" directed against the flag, but did not address other issues associated with state flag desecration laws.

*****

"You're under arrest," four New York policemen shouted as others tried to hold back the growing crowd.

"Damn hippies!" a voice rang out. "Send them to Russia." "Put 'em into Marine boot camp...that'll straighten them out."

"Right on" shouted supporters.

Civil rights activist Sydney Street was burning a flag at the New York intersection of 57th street and 5th Avenue on a Saturday afternoon filled with shoppers. He and his friends were protesting against the shooting of civil rights activist James Meredith in Mississippi.

He was prosecuted under New York's desecration law for *'defiling'* the flag. He was convicted but the higher Court overturned Street's conviction, ruling that verbal disparagement of the flag, one of the charges filed against Street, was protected by the First Amendment. They did not address the issue of flag burning.

Under that state's law a Massachusetts teenager was arrested for wearing a flag patch on the seat of his pants. The Supreme Court ruled that laws vaguely banning *"contempt"* of the flag were unconstitutionally vague and violated the First Amendment's free speech protections. In1974, the Supreme Court ruled that affixing peace sign stickers to a flag is a form of constitutionally protected speech. From all over the country various forms of protest against the government's policies now included creative forms of flag desecration.

Outside the 1984 Republican National Convention in Dallas, Gregory Lee Johnson burned a flag in protest against President Ronald Reagan's policies. The Vietnam War was over but these new more creative methods of civil disobedience remained. Johnson was arrested under Texas' flag desecration statute.

Gregory Lee Johnson was a member of the Revolutionary Communist Youth Brigade, the RCYB. The organization was the former youth group of the Revolutionary Communist Party, USA, founded originally as the *Attica Brigade* before changing its name to the Revolutionary Student Brigade. The RCYB uniform included T-shirts with a large red star superimposed with the silhouette of a young person raising a rifle, some bearing the message, *'I was born in the sewer called capitalism but now I'm living for revolution!'*

The RCYB had been formed several years earlier by Bob Avakian, a Berkeley, California teenager and the son of Armenian immigrants. He later wrote of his high school epiphany:

Bob Avakian

On the way back after a football game I was sitting with some black friends of mine on the team, and we got into this whole deep conversation about why is

there so much racism in this country, why is there
so much prejudice and where does it come from, and
can it ever change, and how could it change? This
was mainly them talking and me listening. And I
remember that very, very deeply – I learned a lot
more in that one hour than I learned in hours of
classroom time, even from some of the better
teachers.

One of the people influenced by Avakian's increasingly militant teachings was Gregory Lee Johnson. He and other demonstrators marched through the streets of Dallas, shouting chants, and brandishing signs outside the offices of several companies. Johnson grabbed an American flag stolen from a flagpole outside one of the targeted buildings. When the demonstrators reached Dallas City Hall, Johnson poured kerosene on the flag and set it on fire. During the burning of the flag, the group shouted such phrases as, *'America, the red, white, and blue, we spit on you, you stand for plunder, you will go under,'* and, *'Reagan, Mondale, which will it be? Either one means World War III.'* No one was hurt, but witnesses to the flag burning said they were extremely offended. One bystander, Daniel E. Walker, received international attention when he collected the burned remains of the flag and buried them according to military protocol in his backyard. The contrasting attitudes of these two men enflamed the public.

Johnson was charged with violating the Texas law that prohibits vandalizing or desecrating respected objects. He was convicted, sentenced to one year in prison, and fined

$2,000. He appealed his conviction to the Fifth Court of Appeals of Texas, but lost the appeal. The Texas Court of Criminal Appeals then reviewed his case. That court overturned his conviction, saying that the State could not punish Johnson for burning the flag because the First Amendment protects such activity as symbolic speech. The Texas Attorney General replied that the state's interests were more important than Johnson's symbolic speech rights because it wanted to preserve the flag as a symbol of national unity, and because it wanted to maintain order. The court disagreed. Neither of these state interests could be used to justify Johnson's conviction, it said. The court also concluded that the flag burning in this case did not cause or threaten to cause a breach of the peace.

'Recognizing that the right to differ is the centerpiece of our First Amendment freedoms, a government cannot mandate by fiat a feeling of unity in its citizens. Therefore, that very same government cannot carve out a symbol of unity and prescribe a set of approved messages to be associated with that symbol. .

The state of Texas appealed to the U.S. Supreme Court!

Gregory Lee 'Joey' Johnson would now be defended by William Kunstler, one of the most incendiary of the liberal attorneys who evolved during this period. Kunstler was a board member of the American Civil Liberties Union, the ACLU, and the co-founder of the Law Center for Constitutional Rights, the CCR, a gathering place for radical lawyers in the country. Kunstler had defended the Black Panthers, the American Indian movement, the Attica prison rioters, and Jack Ruby. He hoped the issue of flag burning would provide him another notch on his liberal pistol.

The question was simple...did the First Amendment, the first, and perhaps, the most important of the Bill of Rights...freedom of speech, apply to non-speech acts as well? Johnson had been convicted of flag desecration rather than any verbal outcries he might have made. Would he be able to invoke the First Amendment to challenge his conviction?

William Kunstler with Gregory Lee Johnson

It was the late 1980's. President Reagan was brandishing his SDI, Space Defense Initiative. Armed American missiles would be placed in outer space under the guise of protecting the United States as they posed a destructive threat to the Soviet Union and the entire globe. The Cold War and the arms race were bankrupting both countries, ultimately forcing the break-up of the Soviet empire. By the end of the decade the Berlin wall, separating the two superpowers would come down. It would begin to unify Europe but the United States continued to be divided.

The Supreme Court had already decided, in previous cases, that displaying a bloodied flag or wearing a black armband could be protected by the First Amendment. That same court had rejected the view that an apparently limitless variety of conduct can be labeled 'speech' whenever the person engaging in the conduct intends to express an idea, but their varied opinions did acknowledge that such conduct may include elements of communication that fall within the scope of the First and Fourteenth Amendments. What was required, they said, was whether *"an intent to convey a particularized message was present, and whether it was likely that the message would be understood by those who viewed it."*

The state defended its statute on two grounds: first, that states had a compelling interest in preserving a venerated national symbol; and second, that the state had a compelling interest in preventing breaches of the peace.

As to the 'breach of the peace', the Court found that "no disturbance of the peace actually occurred or threatened to occur because of Johnson's burning of the flag." The Court also rejected Texas's claim that flag burning was punishable on the basis that it *tends to incite* breaches of the peace, finding that flag burning does not always pose an imminent threat of lawless action. The most contentious issue before the Court, then, was whether states possessed an interest in preserving the flag as a unique symbol of national identity and principles. Texas argued that desecration of the flag impugned its value as such a unique national symbol, and that the state possessed the power to prevent this result.

The court was ideologically divided. Once again there were strict conservative constructionists such as William Rehnquist and Antonin Scalia. There were those who were traditionally more liberal, such as Harry Blackmun and Thurgood Marshall. The remaining five Justices, William Brennan, Anthony Kennedy, Sandra Day O'Conner, John Stevens, and Byron White, moved with the issues. The resolution of this case, however, decided by a single vote, found a different array of conclusions.

Justices Scalia and Kennedy joined Marshall and Blackmun in supporting Justice Brennan's majority opinion:

> *Under the circumstances, Johnson's burning of the flag constituted expressive conduct, permitting him to invoke the First Amendment... Occurring as it did at the end of a demonstration coinciding with the Republican National Convention, the expressive, overtly political nature of the conduct was both intentional and overwhelmingly apparent...the government generally has a freer hand in restricting expressive conduct than it has in restricting the written or spoken word, it may not proscribe particular conduct because it has expressive elements.*

Justice Kennedy, despite considerable pressure from William Rehnquist, supported the majority but wrote a separate concurring opinion:

> *For we are presented with a clear and simple statute to be judged against a pure command of the Constitution. The outcome can be laid at no door but ours. The hard fact is that sometimes we must make decisions we do not like. We make them because they are right...right in the sense that the law and the Constitution, as we see them, compel the result. And so great is our commitment to the process that, except in the rare case, we do not pause to express distaste for the result, perhaps for fear of undermining a valued principle that dictates the decision. This is one of those rare cases. Though symbols often are what we ourselves make of them, the flag is constant in expressing beliefs Americans share, beliefs in law and peace and that freedom which sustains the human spirit. The case here today forces recognition of the costs to which those beliefs commit us. It is poignant but fundamental that the flag protects those who hold it in contempt.*

Chief Justice Rehnquist disagreed vehemently and there was considerable public support for his position:

> *The American flag, then, throughout more than 200 years of our history, has come to be the visible symbol embodying our Nation. It does not represent the views*

of any particular political party, and it does not represent any particular political philosophy. The flag is not simply another "idea" or "point of view" competing for recognition in the marketplace of ideas. Millions and millions of Americans regard it with an almost mystical reverence regardless of what sort of social, political, or philosophical beliefs they may have. I cannot agree that the First Amendment invalidates the Act of Congress, and the laws of 48 of the 50 States, which make criminal the public burning of the flag.

Justice John Paul Stevens also wrote a dissenting opinion. Normally supporting liberal points of view, Justice Stevens argued that the flag

"is more than a proud symbol of the courage, the determination, and the gifts of nature that transformed thirteen fledgling Colonies into a world power. It is a symbol of freedom, of equal opportunity, of religious tolerance, and of good will for other peoples who share our aspirations...The value of the flag as a symbol cannot be measured. This case has nothing to do with 'disagreeable ideas.' It involves disagreeable conduct that diminishes the value of an important national asset."

The Court's majority, however, was clear:

There is, moreover, no indication -either in the text of the Constitution or in our cases interpreting it- that a separate juridical category exists for the American flag alone...We decline, therefore, to create for the flag an exception to the joust of principles protected by the First Amendment.

There is, moreover, no indication -either in the text of the Constitution or in our cases interpreting it- that a separate juridical category exists for the American flag alone...We decline, therefore, to create for the flag an exception to the joust of principles protected by the First Amendment.

Corporate logos instead of stars...was this desecration?

*****

Congress responded immediately by passing a new law, the 1989 Flag Protection Act, making it a federal crime to desecrate the flag. A year later that law was struck down by the same five person majority of justices. Since then, Congress has considered the Flag Desecration Amendment several times. The amendment, sponsored by Utah's Senator Orrin Hatch, a Conservative Republican, has usually been approved by the House of Representatives but the Senate repeatedly rejects it by a substantial margin.

Congress then submitted a new Amendment to the Constitution for approval by two-thirds of the states. The full text of the amendment, passed several times by the U.S. House of Representatives, but always rejected in the Senate reads:

> *The Congress shall have power to prohibit the physical desecration of the flag of the United States.*

The Flag Desecration Amendment was a controversial proposal that would prohibit expression of political views through the physical desecration of the flag of the United States. The concept of flag desecration continues to provoke a heated debate over protecting a national symbol, protecting free speech, and protecting the liberty represented by a national symbol. While the proposed amendment most frequently refers to 'flag burning,' the language would permit the prohibition of all forms of flag desecration, which could take forms other than burning, such as using the flag for clothing or napkins. In 2006 the United States Senate rejected the Amendment, by one vote short of the two-thirds majority it necessary to pass the Amendment to the states for their concurrence. The House had approved it by a wide margin and leading Democrats and Republicans in the Senate urged its passage. The vote would be close. A national poll showed that 56% of Americans supported the Amendment.

Arlen Spector, Senior Senator from Pennsylvania and head of the Judiciary Committee that approved the Amendment and sent it to the full Senate, made his opinions clear, "Flag desecration is similar to libel and child pornography. They are forms of expression that have no social value. Flag burning is a form of expression that is spiteful or vengeful. It is designed to hurt. It is not designed to persuade."

The Democrats loudest voice opposing passage was Senator Leahy from Vermont...we must not limit free speech, he championed. Leave it to the Courts to determine what desecration is. In the end Leahy's arguments held sway. Three Republicans joined him and the Amendment was defeated.

Freedom of speech, the bulwark of the Bill of Rights, remained sacrosanct, thanks to a single vote.

XI

RELIGIOUS FREEDOM

The first Amendment to the U.S. Constitution boldly avers that "Congress shall make no law respecting an establishment of religion, or prohibiting the free exercise thereof." This small group of radical colonial thinkers, many of whom had left their homes across Europe to practice religion as their conscience dictated, agreed to forever sever any relation between God and government...or almost. On currency and in their hearts, they proclaimed *"In God We Trust."* Prayers opened the meetings of Congress and the relationship of church and state ebbed and flowed through the country's history

*****

There was still snow above the 6,000 foot elevation as Guy Ballard struggled to follow a trail whose signs were barely visible beneath a whirling white blanket. An early morning haze drifted lazily around him and in the cold air he could see his breath. Ballard had risen at dawn, heated water for some tea and filled his canteen with water. It was the same one he had carried in the trenches of France during World War I. Without admitting it, he thought of it as a lucky talisman. He put on his gloves and parka, and headed up the mountain. It was early spring 1930 and Guy Ballard, mining engineer, and student of the occult, believed Mount Shasta, in

California's Sierra Nevada Mountains, was filled with religious significance.

He didn't get down from his hilly trek until the late afternoon sun was already depositing length shadows and the temperature had begun to drop. He piled everything into his Model A and pressed the gas pedal to the floorboard. He was filled with awe and excitement and eager to share his adventure.

Guy Ballard

"Edna," he said to his wife, rushing, out of breath, into their small bungalow. "I met a man on the trail this afternoon who called himself Saint Germain. We sat together for hours. I hadn't seen him while I was climbing. I just suddenly turned and there he was. He didn't really seem dressed for the weather but I couldn't take my eyes off him. He exuded a warmth and a comfort I've never felt before. He spoke in a quiet voice with just the hint of an accent. He was the most unusual and miraculous man I'd ever seen. He explained life's purpose to me... imagine, finally understanding our purpose and the life after that awaits us. He said that I was to be his messenger."

Four years later Ballard published his first book, *Unveiled Mysteries*, where he introduced the concept of the Ascended Master. Ballard asserted that the contents of his book and the philosophies they espoused had been dictated to him by the 'Ascended Master,' Saint Germain, the man who had spoken to him on the mountain. The primary tenet was that the presence of a Life/God individualizes as the *"I AM"*, and flows throughout the universe until it achieves an *'Ascension' ...a mastery through enlightenment.'* Ballard proclaimed that Saint Germain had named him to be such a messenger, able to provide intuitive, inspired interpretations...a raised and purified outer self with the *"I AM"* presence, a true identity that is the unique individualization of Almighty God for each person.

Ballard's *"I AM"* activities and converts grew from his lectures about Saint Germain's mystical teachings. During the depression myriads of people, out of work and hungry, were searching for some meaning to explain their despondency. By 1938, there may have been as many as a million followers in the United States. But in 1939, even as his teachings continued to attract more and more attention, Guy Ballard died from natural causes, not in the ascendant manner he had always proclaimed. Edna ignored the confusion. His body was cremated as his wife declared his 'ascension,' in a manner similar to Jesus. Guy Ballard had entered heaven alive and now sat at the right hand of the original Ascendant Master, Saint Germain.

Edna Ballard and her son, Donald, continued to preach the "*I AM*" theology. Three years later, and despite the nation's focus on the war effort, they were indicted in California on eighteen counts of fraud. The indictment charged that the Ballards fraudulently collected over $3 million from their followers on the basis of religious claims the Ballards knew were false. Their followers protested outside the courthouse and San Francisco police were posted to prevent violence as the pair's trial got underway.

The judges of the Federal District Court instructed the jury to convict the pair if they found that the Ballards did not have a good faith belief in their religious claims. It was a test of the First Amendment to the Constitution. What defined a religion? Who would determine whether claims of an afterlife that were not part of an already established religion were valid or fantasy? The Ballards were convicted on all counts and appealed the finding to the Ninth Circuit Court of Appeals. That court overturned the conviction and the government appealed. The case of the *United States v. Ballard* would now be heard by the Supreme Court.

The nine members of the Court were not doctrinaire. It was 1944 and they, like the rest of Americans, were more interested in the D-Day invasion and the battles in the Pacific. President Franklin Roosevelt was running for an unprecedented fourth term and the country was unified and patriotic. Ideas that strayed from such patriotism were unpopular.

In a 5-4 landmark decision, the court ruled that the question of whether the Ballards believed their religious claims should not have been submitted to the jury. In his majority opinion, Justice William Douglas wrote:

> *The religious views espoused by the Ballards might seem incredible, if not preposterous, to most people. But if those doctrines are subject to trial before a jury charged with finding their truth or falsity, then the same can be done with the religious beliefs of any sect. When the triers of fact undertake that task, they enter a forbidden domain. The First Amendment does not select any one group or any one type of religion for preferred treatment. It puts them all in that position.*

Justice William O. Douglas

Four justices joined him but Justice Harlan Stone dissented, joined by Justices Felix Frankfurter and Owen Roberts.

I am not prepared to say that the constitutional guarantee of freedom of religion affords immunity from criminal prosecution for the fraudulent procurement of money by false statements as to one's religious experiences, more than it renders polygamy or libel immune from criminal prosecution... I cannot say that freedom of thought and worship includes freedom to procure money by making knowingly false statements about one's religious experiences.

Justice Robert Jackson also dissented, but for a different reason.

I should say the defendants have done just that for which they are indicted. If I might agree to their conviction without creating a precedent, I cheerfully would do so. I can see in their teachings nothing but humbug, untainted by any trace of truth. But that does not dispose of the constitutional question whether misrepresentation of religious experience or belief is prosecutable; it rather emphasizes the danger of such prosecutions. Prosecutions of this character easily could degenerate into religious persecution. I would dismiss the indictment and have done with this business of judicially examining other people's faiths. All schools of religious thought make enormous assumptions, generally on the basis of revelations authenticated by some sign or miracle. Some who profess belief in the Bible read literally what others read as allegory or metaphor, as they read Aesop's fables.

If we try religious sincerity severed from religious verity, we isolate the dispute from the very considerations which, in common experience, provide its most reliable answer. William James, who wrote on these matters as a scientist, reminds us that it is not theology and ceremonies which keep religion going. Its vitality is in the religious experiences of many people. "If you ask what these experiences are, they are conversations with the unseen, voices and visions, responses to prayer, changes of heart, deliverances from fear, inflowings of help, assurances of support, whenever certain persons set their own internal attitude in certain appropriate ways."

By a 5-4 decision…a single vote, a definition of religious freedom had been established. But that invisible line would be repeatedly tested.

*****

"For God's sake, how can you object? That's the Ten Commandments we're displaying."

"That's why!"

Whitley City, Kentucky, home of eleven hundred warm bodies in the 2000 census, 99% of whom were white, is also the McReary County seat. It boasts a pleasant Court house at which they chose to display in a bold and ornate fashion, copies of the Ten Commandments. In 2004 the ACLU took issue with the display and filed suit to have it removed as a violation of the U.S. Constitution's First Amendment espousing a relationship between government and religion. After the suit was filed the displays around the Commandments were modified to include eight smaller, historical documents containing religious references as their sole common element, such as the Declaration of Independence's *endowed by their Creator* passage. County officials defended their displays as a commemoration of historical documents rather than a religious motivation.

The District Court followed a principle, colloquially called the *Lemon test,* from a 1971 Supreme Court Case, *Lemon v. Kurtzman,* which detailed the requirements for determining such questions. The Court concluded that were three considerations:

1. *The government's action **must have a secular legislative purpose**;*

2. *The government's action **must not have the primary effect of either advancing or inhibiting religion**;*

3. *The government's action* **must not result in an**
    "excessive government entanglement" *with*
    religion.

If any of these were violated, the government's action was
to be deemed unconstitutional under the Establishment
Clause of the First Amendment to the United States
Constitution.

The court determined that McReary County's display
lacked any secular purpose. The County had tried, several
times, to revise the exhibit. Each revision failed to change the
lower court's opinion.   The exhibit was now titled 'The
Foundations of American Law and Government Display.'   It
consisted of nine framed documents of equal size. The Ten
Commandment display explicitly identified it as being from
the King James Version of the New Testament. It quoted
paragraphs at length, explaining how it had influenced the
formation of Western legal thought and America's formation.
Next to the Ten Commandments were framed copies of the
Star Spangled Banner's lyrics and the Declaration of
Independence, accompanied by statements about their
historical and legal significance.   Once again the court
rejected the County's reasoning. The Commandments were
religious rather than secular. The U.S. Circuit Court affirmed
the decision, and the Supreme Court agreed to hear the
matter.

"I want you to file a law suit on my behalf." Thomas Van
Orden had walked into the Austin, Texas offices of the ACLU

and shouted his demand. Van Orden was a derelict, homeless, unshaven, clothes wrinkled, and dirty from sleeping on park benches when he couldn't get a room at a shelter. Four years earlier he had been a practicing attorney but he had been suspended for misconduct. Now he spent his days wandering around the Austin Court House.

A sympathetic attorney offered him coffee and listened, distressed at the condition of this man he had once heard mesmerize a jury. Van Orden convinced the man and local ACLU to file a law suit regarding the display of the Ten Commandments on a monument given to the government and prominently displayed on the grounds surrounding the government buildings. The case of Van Orden v. Perry began its trek through the courts. Perry, Governor of Texas, had been named as Plaintiff in the suit. Lower courts had decided such displays were constitutional on the grounds the display conveyed both a religious and a secular message. This particular monument was 6-feet high and 3-feet wide. It had been donated to the State of Texas in 1961 by the Fraternal Order of Eagles, a civic organization, with the support of Cecil B. DeMille, famed movie director of the film *The Ten Commandments*.

The State accepted the monument and selected a site for it based on the recommendation of the state agency responsible for maintaining the Capitol grounds. The donating organization paid the cost of erecting the display. Two state legislators presided over the dedication of the area. It was situated on the Capitol grounds, surrounded by twenty-two acres that contained seventeen other monuments and twenty-one historical markers commemorating the *'people, ideals, and events that compose Texan identity.'*

And, on the same day the court released its 5-4 decision on the McCreary case deciding that the display was primarily religious in nature and violated the First Amendment, it released a completely opposite 5-4 vote, deciding that the Texas display was constitutional. The clarity of the opinion rendered in the Ballard case had now been lost in simultaneous conflicting decisions

Justice Stephen Breyer had concurred and voted with the court's majority in the decision that the displaying of the Ten Commandments in front of a Kentucky Court House violated the First Amendment. He had not written a separate opinion. In the Texas case, however, Justice Breyer decided that the Texas display of the same Ten Commandments did NOT violate the First Amendment. This time he chose to write a separate but concurring statement:

> The case before us is a borderline case. It concerns a large granite monument bearing the text of the Ten Commandments located on the grounds of the Texas State Capitol. On the one hand, the Commandments' text undeniably has a religious message, invoking, indeed emphasizing, the Deity. On the other hand, focusing on the text of the Commandments alone cannot conclusively resolve this case. Rather, to

determine the message that the text here conveys, we must examine how the text is used. And that inquiry requires us to consider the context of the display.

Justice Stephen Breyer

He then proceeded to justify his logic for determining whether the display had a sufficient 'secular purpose,' including the following:

1. *The monument's 40-year history on the Texas state grounds indicates that nonreligious aspects of the tablets' message predominate.*

2. *The group that donated the monument, the Fraternal Order of Eagles, is a private civic (and primarily secular) organization. Who, while interested in the religious aspect of the Ten Commandments, sought to highlight the Commandments' role in shaping civic morality as part of that organization's efforts to combat juvenile delinquency.*

3. *The Eagles' consulted with a committee composed of members of several faiths in order to find a nonsectarian text — an act which underscores the group's ethics-based motives.*

4. *The tablets, as displayed on the monument, prominently acknowledge that the Eagles donated the display.*

5. *The physical setting of the monument suggests little or nothing of the sacred.*

    a. The monument sits in a large park containing 17 monuments and 21 historical markers, all designed to illustrate the "ideals" of those who settled in Texas and of those who have lived there since that time.

    b. The setting does not readily lend itself to meditation or any other religious activity.

    c. The setting does provide a context of history and moral ideals.

    d. The larger display (together with the display's inscription about its origin) communicates to visitors that the State sought to reflect moral principles, illustrating a relation between ethics and law that the State's citizens, historically speaking, have endorsed. That is to say, the context suggests that the State intended the display's moral message — an illustrative message reflecting the historical "ideals" of Texans — to predominate.

In Justice Breyer's book, In *Active Liberty*, he argued that the framers of the Constitution sought to establish a democratic government involving the maximum liberty for its citizens. He repeatedly referenced another book that spoke of '*freedom from government coercion*' and '*freedom to participate in the government.*' He championed a philosophy of 'active liberty' in which a judge always opined on the side of protecting the democratic intentions of the Constitution.

His single vote denying the legality of one display, while approving another, demonstrated his desire to achieve a balance between secular messages of morality and those that tread too closely to religion.

XII

THE 2000 DISPUTED ELECTION OF GEORGE W. BUSH

In the pre-dawn hours of a cold, moonless night in late November 1999, on the outskirts of the small village of Cardenas on Cuba's north shore, fourteen people crowded into a small aluminum boat, powered by a single engine that would unexpectedly prove to be faulty. Their destination, like so many others before them, was to escape from Socialist Cuba for the opportunity of a better life that lay ninety miles across the sea. They were following the path of nearly one million people...lawyers, doctors, professors, and rural campesinos, who shared the dream of 'La Yuma,' the Cuban slang word for the United States. They had chosen this night carefully. Cuban shore patrols were alert to those who wanted to leave and abandon their responsibilities to Fidel Castro and his revolution. The boat had been hidden earlier in the day in the hidden crevices and bushes along the marshy shore. Thirteen Cubans had taken off their shoes to cross the damp sand. The fourteenth, a young toddler, Elián Gonzales, was only six years old. He was wrapped in a blanket, half-asleep, and carried by his mother's boyfriend, Lazaro Garcia. Elián's mother, twenty-eight year old Elizabet Brotons Rodriguez, had separated from the boy's father, Juan Quintana, two years earlier. Juan had been her first 'novio,' her first sweetheart. They had married young, neither prepared for the responsibility of raising a child.

234

Elizabet worked as a maid in a tourist hotel and, by Cuban standards, made a small, but decent income. She loved her son, she had a new boyfriend, and her mother, who lived close by was able to help.

What compelled her to board the small boat that night isn't clear. She knew the passage was dangerous and she was risking the lives of both she and her son. Perhaps it was Lazaro's idea...a chance to start a new life together. Another mother, Arianne Horta Alfonso, made a last minute decision and left her five year old daughter behind out of concern for the young girl's safety on such a dangerous crossing.

The small cluster of shipmates was excited with their adventure and the dreams of what awaited them in Florida. As their boat cleared the incoming waves, one of the men pointed the bow northwest. He understood that Gulf currents would push them east and he needed to counteract them, but an hour out their engine failed and the boat began taking on water. It was a new peril they hadn't anticipated.

An unexpected squall engulfed them. Waves of more than ten feet battered their boat and they were unable to get the engine restarted. They were without power and at the mercy of the weather. Two of the men had the foresight to attach inner tubes to the back of the boat but without a motor to keep their craft moving forward, both the boat and the inner tubes began to fill with the sea's cold water.

Elizabet put her sweater around her shivering young son and Lazaro set him carefully in one of the inner tubes that he'd drained of the encroaching water.

"No matter what, take care of Elián. See that he makes it to land," his mother shouted over the rain that was buffeting them. They were her last words. Only three people survived the journey, Ariane Alfonso, who had left her young daughter on the beach, Nivaldo Ferran, a male passenger, and Elián, tucked into an inner tube, asleep.

As the sun peaked above the horizon a small fishing boat spotted the tiny stalled craft. Elián was still in the inner tube, cold, soaking, crying and frightened. Nivaldo and Ariane were treading water, clinging to the overturned boat. They were certain they would die there. Ariane was happy she had decided to leave her daughter in Cardenas but she was filled with the tragic feeling that she'd never see her little girl again. These were not the first Cubans the fishermen had picked up. The remnants of failed expectations could be seen by the broken boats piled up along the docks of Key West.

The man, woman and young child were wrapped in blankets and given hot cups of coffee. The small trawler turned back toward Florida where they could make radio contact with a U.S. Coast Guard boat patrolling the area. There would be no fish today. Instead, like so many times over these past years, they had netted a dire human cargo.

After seeing to the well-being of the three survivors, the Coast Guard boat headed quickly for American land where all three would be turned over to the Immigration and Naturalization Service, the INS. The little boy was released to his paternal great-uncle, Lázaro, who lived in the Cuban expat enclave of Miami. Juan Quintana, Elián's birth father, had telephoned Lázaro from Cuba to advise him that Elizabet and Elián had left Cuba without his knowledge, and to watch for their arrival.

"Donde esta mi madre?" Elián asked, the next morning, waking in a different bed in a different room. Where is my mother? How does one explain to a little boy, not quite six years old, that his mother was gone and he was now ninety miles away with strangers who smiled at him, fed him and fussed over him?

"Mi abuela. Quiero mi abuela," the little boy cried. If his mother wasn't there, he needed his grandmother who often cared for him. But she, too, was absent, crying for the loss of her daughter and grandson back in Cardenas. For three decades those who had fled to a sanctuary in the United States were as distant as if they'd traveled to the moon. The old woman might never see her grandson, Elián, again.

*****

Hostility between Cuba and the United States had been persistent since Fidel Castro, Che Guevara, and their supporters ousted the violent military rule of General Juan Batista, the Mafia's gambling empire, and the American investors who controlled the island's sugar and tobacco industries in the late 1950's. Castro, the fatigue-wearing, cigar-chomping, revolutionary, had proclaimed socialist equality for all Cubans and began a massive redistribution of income. Prosperous and professional Cubans took what they could and streamed across the water for the United States. Initially this emigration was illegal under both Cuban and U.S. law. Cubans found at sea, attempting to reach what they hoped would be friendlier shores, would be deported by the U.S. Coast Guard or, if discovered by Cuban forces, would be returned to the island, their assets forfeited to the state.

Denied trade with the United States, Cuba turned to the Soviet Union for support. When this support included the installation of Russian missiles pointed toward the United States, the world poised for the threat of a nuclear war. For days the world awaited the resolution of 'the Cuban Missile Crisis.' It was nuclear brinksmanship as three Soviet ships sped across the Atlantic Ocean toward the island. War seemed imminent until the Soviets agreed to turn their ships around. The world sighed in relief.

The combination of the missile crisis and internal problems forced the Soviet Union to end its support for Fidel. Turmoil on the island continued. Educated middle-class and professionals, restricted from leaving, wanted more for their children. Between late 1960 and late 1962 more than 14,000 young children, boys and girls not yet in their teens, were sent away from their families and friends in Cuba to live with family members in the United States. Their parents were afraid that their children were going to be sent to some Soviet bloc countries to be educated and they decided to send them to the States as soon as possible. It was the beginning of what would be more than one million Cubans leaving their country, angry…vowing to return.

The small island was a thorn in the paw of U.S. policy. Eight years earlier, in 1961, CIA-trained Cuban émigrés, with American military support, attempted to retake the island by force and oust Castro. Guerilla forces invaded the island at the Bay of Pigs, only to face the superior forces of the Cuban Army.   It was an embarrassing failure as Fidel's forces captured the invaders. Thousands of Cuban émigrés would continue to remain in south Florida, separated from parents, families, and friends.

The United States adopted a policy that came to be described as a 'wet feet, dry feet' rule.   Any Cuban citizen picked up at sea, or walking toward shore, ("wet feet") would be returned to the island.

If they made it to shore ("dry feet"), they would be permitted political asylum and allowed to remain in the United States. In 1966 passage of the Cuban Adjustment Act allowed those who had arrived to apply for U.S. residency.

*****

The early months of 2000 saw the United States continuing an unprecedented period of prosperity. The Y2K 'bug' had come and gone without incident. The NASDAQ reached an all-time high. The country was euphoric as it entered a new millennium. But the yin and the yang, the good and the bad of the world, continued.

Despite fears of interruption to shipping, the Panama Canal had been transferred without incident to the Panamanian government a few months earlier. But there was also sadness as the last Peanuts cartoon was printed following the death of Charles Schulz. The rest of the world continued its ongoing turmoil. There was growing violence in the old Yugoslavia, now facing conflicting claims and abuses by Serbs, Croats and Bosnians. Vladimir Putin was elected President of Russia while torrential floods killed 800 in Mozambique.

Names that dominated the public's fascination in early 1999 as the country awaited the impeachment trial of the President...the first since Andrew Johnson more than one hundred years earlier, had faded from the stand-up routines of late night comedians. Monica Lewinsky, Linda Tripp, and Paula Jones, as well as taped private conversations, definitions of sexual intercourse, and innuendos that were cannon fodder for tabloids and 24-hour news reporting were no longer lead stories but the repeated embarrassments and diversions had destroyed the President's effectiveness. The charisma that swept him into office would not be available to support the next Democratic nominee.

Presidential politics in the United States begins the day after the previous election and, with an incumbent President unable to run for re-election, the 2000 contest would be no different.

Al Gore, Vice-President, and former Senator from Tennessee, was the undisputed contender for the Democratic nomination. He was tall, handsome, with a photogenic wife and family. But he wasn't Bill Clinton. President Clinton...smiling, politically astute, saxophone-playing, and sexually attractive, was the man from Hope, Arkansas, with the intelligent, equally savvy wife. He had played the political center as deftly as Stan Getz played jazz sax. He had balanced the Federal budget for the first time in decades and he might have been named a political saint had it not been for his sexual gaffes. Gore would have to face the electorate on his own, burdened by Clinton's negatives, unable to take advantage of his predecessor's positive accomplishments.

Vice-President Al Gore

The Republican Party had no such certain nominee. Their political field was crowded...it was anyone's race. The leading hopeful was Senator John McCain of Arizona. He had been a Navy pilot, Vietnam War hero, and prisoner of war. He was a well-known and popular moderate in the party. Steve Forbes, multi-millionaire publisher of Forbes magazine and son of its founder, Malcolm Forbes, entered the race to push his agenda of a 'flat tax.'

Senator Orrin Hatch, the senior Senator from Utah was the nation's most prominent Mormon. Elizabeth Dole, wife of Senator Bob Dole, and President of the American Red Cross, was equally well known. Dan Quayle, Vice-President under George Herbert Bush, also wanted the nomination. From the far conservative right of the party were Pat Buchanan, radio commentator and publisher, and Alan Keyes, a United Nations representative under President Reagan and one of the few African-American faces in the party. Two other dark horses were also in the field, Governor Lamar Alexander from Tennessee, and George W. Bush, son of the former President and Governor of Texas. The campaign was well under way by early 2000.

The Republican primary season began with an Iowa straw poll in January that favored George W. Bush. The Iowa farmers were angered by John McCain's reluctance to grant Federal subsidies on using corn for ethanol. The first serious primary was New Hampshire; McCain won handily. It was clear that young Bush had hurdled most of the rest of the field. He had his father's name recognition and, more importantly, his father's money and organization.

George W. Bush

Bush took most of the southern state primaries while McCain won sizeable victories in Michigan and his home state of Arizona. George Bush won California and Washington. Bush campaign slurs against his opponent accelerated, *'John McCain's adopted Bangladeshi daughter is actually black.' 'McCain is gay and cheats on his wife.' 'His wife Cindy is a drug addict.' 'His five years as a prisoner of war in North Vietnam drove him insane.' 'McCain committed treason while a prisoner of war, and fathered a child by a black prostitute.'* All accusations seemed to be the brain-child of political strategist, Carl Rove, master Republican tactician, and they came with machine-gun rapidity wherever McCain was set to appear. Whatever message the veteran Senator hoped to convey was muted.

As the last days of July were torn from the calendar, the humidity in Philadelphia was record-breaking and the results of the Republican convention being held there had become a fait accompli. Weeks earlier, a frustrated John McCain had sparred with the Christian Right in South Carolina, and lost. Bush and Rove's negative campaign had exhausted him. He had been a Navy pilot and a hero. Accusations of being gay or conspiring with the enemy were bad, accusations against his wife and children were false and malicious. He was emotionally drained.

George W. Bush's message of *'compassionate conservatism'* rang through the hall as he stood there in early August with his running mate, Dick Cheney, their arms locked together, and upraised, as they celebrated their victory. They had swept the voting. Al Gore and the return to a Republican White House were now in their sights.

In recent decades much of the American electorate had become firmly entrenched in one party or the other. The large liberal states, most with 'winner take all' elections, such as California, New York, and Pennsylvania, typically ended up in the 'blue' Democratic column. The southern states that had voted as a Democratic bloc since the Civil War had shifted during the Civil Rights movement of the '60's and were now Republican 'red' states. Rural, laissez-faire mid-west states voted 'red'; northeast and Pacific coast states, 'blue.' The elections often resolved around the swing states of Florida, Michigan, Ohio, and Illinois. That's where the political struggle would be the most intense.

*****

The battle over Elián had been ongoing since late January when both his grandmothers flew to the United States from

Havana seeking the return of their grandson to Cuban soil. Their pleas were rejected by the boy's great grand uncle, who was adamant that Elián remain in the United States. He finally acquiesced to allowing the Cuban women to see their grandson.

The uncle hoped he could convince the women that the boy would have a better life if he remained in Florida. The child had become a political 'football.' The women took their case to Washington and met with Attorney General Janet Reno. Media coverage had reached a frenzied stage and Republicans, eager to capitalize on the issue, tried to pass a special bill giving the child U.S. citizenship. Their efforts failed and the two elderly women sobbed openly in front of the cameras as they were forced to return to Cuba without Elián.

International pressure mounted. The Spanish Foreign Minister called for the boy's return. "International law dictates the child's return," he said. Meanwhile, Elián's Miami family was accused of offering the boy's natural father substantial money if he abandoned the action and joined his son in Miami. Juan Quintana refused and continued his efforts from Cuba to get his son returned. He wrote open letters that were published in Cuban newspapers and reprinted in papers across the United States. It was a story that captivated both countries and symbolized in a single relationship the shredding of thousands of families on both sides of the water's divide.

In Miami, Elián was a cause célèbre and the Gonzalez family cared for him and loved him unabashedly. His presence in defiance of Castro's government was a tiny victory...but it was something. They petitioned for asylum for the boy but the Federal court denied it.

The entire Miami Cuban community joined the effort to keep the boy in the United States. Civic leaders indicated that their city would not cooperate with Federal authorities on any attempt to repatriate the boy nor would they lend police or other assistance. In April, a video was released in which Elián tells his Cuban father that he wants to remain in the United States. It was evident the young boy had been coached repeatedly in what to say.

The Democratic administration was being forced by the courts to follow the law and Al Gore was trapped. He initially supported Republican legislation to give the boy and his father permanent residence status, but then changed to support the Administration position. He was attacked both for pandering and being inconsistent. The Republicans, facing no responsibility in the final outcome, and pandering to the Cuban community, supported efforts to keep Elián in the United States.

In mid-April, the 11th Circuit Court of Appeals in Atlanta ruled that Elián remain until his Miami family could appeal for an asylum hearing in May. In late April, however, Attorney General Janet Reno ordered the return of the young boy to his father in Cuba. The Miami relatives defied the order. Negotiations between the two sides continued while the home where Elián had been living was surrounded around the clock by protesters committed to keeping the boy in the United States as well as police hoping to avoid violence.

Elián's relatives insisted on assurances that they could live with the child for several more months and that the boy would not be returned to Cuba. They were unable to reach any workable solution. Meanwhile, a Florida family court judge revoked Lázaro's temporary custody, clearing the way for Elián to be returned to the custody of his birth father. Attorney General Reno made the decision to remove Elián from the house and instructed law enforcement officials to determine the best time to obtain the boy. There were fears that those in the house might be heavily armed. There was no question that the family would use any means to keep Elián from being returned to a Cuba they hated.

In the pre-dawn hours of April 22, pursuant to an order issued by a federal magistrate, eight SWAT-equipped agents of an elite Border Patrol unit joined more than 130 INS agents. They approached the house, knocked, and identified themselves. When no one responded from within, they entered the house. Crowds outside the house threw rocks and bottles in an attempt to thwart the boy's seizure as the agents responded, firing canisters of pepper-spray and mace.

Armando Gutierrez, a prominent spokesman for the Cuban émigrés, was in the house and had smuggled in an

Associated Press photographer. They waited in the room with Elián and family members, listening to agents searching the house. A widely publicized photograph of a border patrol agent, pointing an automatic weapon at Elián and the man holding him, hiding in a closet, cascaded across the front pages of newspapers around the world. A Democratic Attorney General and the Democratic President, who had appointed her, were bullies, frightening a young boy and thwarting the hopes of a million Cubans.

Elián being removed at gunpoint from his Relative's home in Miami

Agents found that more than two dozen protesters had concealed weapons. "Assassins!" the crowd yelled, as they continued their futile rampage. Within an hour of the raid, crowds in Little Havana tripled in size, pouring out in the street, overturning cars and trash cans, jamming a ten-block area as police in riot gear were deployed, using tear gas to break up the demonstrations.

"What now, Armando?" the elder Lázaro asked, his grand nephew gone, as he and his wife sat crying, their house and furnishings nearly destroyed by the rush of the Federal agents. "They have taken Elián back to that cursed Fidel."

The area around the house had become eerily quiet. The protesters had left and moved into the central area where they joined others in wreaking havoc on local businesses.

"Our battle is not over," Armando said, putting his arm around his elderly friend. "We will show them that the Cubans in this country matter. We will create a political tsunami that makes politicians listen to us. If we had been a bigger force, this would never have happened."

*****

Each of the prior three decades had seen the state of Florida grow by more than three million. The state's 1990 population was thirteen million...in 2000 it was sixteen million, eleven million of which were eligible voters. In the 1996 election, however, less than six million people actually voted.

The Hispanic portion of the electorate had grown to exceed 15% and two-thirds of that was Cuban, the remainder was Puerto Rican, Mexican or from Latin America. Most of the Cubans, Castro's émigrés, lived in South Miami's 'Little Havana.' In Miami's Dade County, Cubans represented more than 50% of all eligible voters. The state supported Bill Clinton for President in 1996 despite its inherent Republican leanings. The Cuban activists weren't going to make that mistake again.

The campaign continued...the vitriol grew. Bill Clinton's mantra *'it's the economy, stupid'* was no longer the primary issue. The economy was sound and domestic issues such as reforms of Social Security and Medicare, and competing plans for tax relief, received little public attention.

Bush criticized the Democrat's involvement in Somalia where eighteen American soldiers died in 1993 trying to sort out warring factions. U.S. troops were also in the Balkans, trying to keep Bosnians, Serbs, and Croats from killing one another.

"I don't think our troops ought to be used for what's called nation-building," Bush said in the second presidential debate. "I will also pledge to bridge partisan gaps that stand in the way of progress on necessary reforms." He also promised to return 'integrity' to the White House, a clear reference to Bill Clinton's peccadilloes in the Oval Office.

Al Gore hammered on George Bush's fitness for the job, pointing to gaffes made by Bush in interviews and speeches and suggesting the Texas governor lacked the necessary experience to be president.

Both candidates had to deal with controversy on their flanks. Al Gore continued to avoid appearing with Clinton, even in states where the sitting President remained popular. This offended a significant segment of the liberal wing of the party and many sat on their hands, unwilling to get out the vote for their party. Other disaffected Democrats turned to Ralph Nader, long-time liberal icon, who was also on the ballot in several swing states. Meanwhile, Ross Perot, an outspoken Republican conservative, was draining votes from George Bush. As fall leaves turned brown and covered the ground, and children put away their Halloween costumes, the race was too close to call.

Bush v. Gore

The night of the election, the entire country was riveted. Some states and parts of the country were resolved early. George Bush carried all the southern states except Gore's home state of Tennessee. Florida remained in doubt. George Bush also won Ohio, Indiana and much of the mid-west. Al Gore swept California, the northwest and most of New England.

By early morning all the states except New Mexico, Oregon, and Florida were decided. Neither New Mexico's nor Oregon's electoral votes would decide the election one way or the other. At this point George Bush had 246 electoral votes...Al Gore 255; 270 were needed to win. It would all come down to Florida's twenty-five votes. Both New Mexico and Oregon would be won by Gore but Florida's results were a mess.

On November 8, two days after the election, the Florida Division of Elections reported that George Bush was the declared winner with 48.8% of the vote in Florida, beating Al Gore by 1,784 votes. Ralph Nader may have siphoned off enough votes to alter the decision. The Cuban community had increased its voter registration by 81%. Armando Gutierrez had kept his promise. The overwhelming number of Cuban voters and their anger at the Democrats was having a major effect in Florida's election results.

When the margin of victory was less than 0.5% of the votes cast, however, it forced a statutorily-mandated automatic machine recount. Two days later the machine recount was finished in all but one county, Bush's margin had decreased to 327. On races this close, candidates are allowed to demand a manual recount but Florida law also specified that the manual recount had to take place within seven days, an impossible requirement for everything except local races. In the largest, normally Democratic counties, Court challenges flowed...enter Katherine Harris, Florida's Secretary of State, appointed by Jeb Bush, the state's Governor and George Bush's brother.   Ms. Harris was an ambitious woman, anxious to move up within the party and she vigorously defended any rule which would lead to a Bush-Cheney victory.

Recounts took place and a new word entered the lexicon... 'hanging chad,' the tiny piece of a punched card that fails to fully drop off when a hole is punched.   Claims of vote tampering, statistically unlikely results, and an inability to complete tasks on time continued.   Harris would permit no extension of the recount deadline.   Her office completed the counting of absentee ballots and she announced that George Bush had won the election in Florida.

Thanksgiving came and went, Christmas shopping was in full swing but the decision on who would be the next President was still unresolved.   In early December the Florida Supreme Court, by a 4-3 vote, ordered a statewide manual recount, but a day later, the U.S. Supreme Court intervened on a vote of 5-4 to stayed the Florida recount.   According to Justice Scalia, writing for the majority:

"The issuance of the stay suggests that a majority of the Court, while not deciding the issues presented, believe that the petitioner (Bush) has a substantial probability of success. The issue is not, as the dissent puts it, whether "counting every legally cast vote can constitute irreparable harm." One of the principal issues in the appeal we have accepted is precisely whether the votes that

have been ordered to be counted are, under a reasonable interpretation of Florida law, "legally cast votes." The counting of votes that are of questionable legality does in my view threaten irreparable harm to petitioner Bush, and to the country, by casting a cloud upon what he claims to be the legitimacy of his election. Count first, and rule upon legality afterwards, is not a recipe for producing election results that have the public acceptance democratic stability requires."

The four dissenting Judges disagreed: "Counting every legally cast vote cannot constitute irreparable harm... Preventing the recount from being completed will inevitably cast a cloud on the legitimacy of the election." They argued that stopping the recount was an "unwise" violation of "three venerable rules of judicial restraint", namely respecting the opinions of state supreme courts, cautiously exercising jurisdiction when "another branch of the Federal Government" has a large measure of responsibility to resolve the issue, and avoiding making peremptory conclusions on federal constitutional questions.

At this point, the composition of the Supreme Court came into question. Four of the justices had been appointed by Republican Presidents and were considered quite conservative: Antonin Scalia, Clarence Thomas, Anthony Kennedy, and Sandra Day O'Conner. On the more liberal side were Ruth Bader Ginsburg, Steven Breyer, and John Paul

Stevens. William Rehnquist, Chief Justice, as usual, was the pivotal vote.

Justice Rehnquist was a conservative ideologue. He favored an interpretation of federalism that emphasized the Constitution's Tenth Amendment that reserved the powers to the states. He had served on the Court longer than all but three other justices. Other justices often criticized his "willingness to cut corners to reach a conservative result", "glossing over inconsistencies of logic or fact" or distinguishing indistinct cases to reach his predetermined conclusion. Similarly, he was often accused of being contemptuous of the opinions of more liberal judges, accusing them of "bending the facts or law to suit their purposes."

The Court's first ruling, in a 7-2 vote, was that the Florida Supreme Court's decision, calling for a statewide recount, violated the Equal Protection Clause of the Fourteenth Amendment. "Even if the recount was fair in theory, it was unfair in practice," they wrote. "The evidence suggests that different standards were applied to the recount from ballot to ballot, precinct to precinct, and county to county, even when identical types of ballots and machines were used."

But then the justices ruled 5–4 that no constitutionally valid recount could be completed by the December

12th,"safe harbor," deadline. "The Supreme Court of Florida has said that the legislature intended the State's electors to 'participate fully in the federal electoral process", and, therefore, the date could not be extended."

The four liberal justices were vehement in their objections. The Supreme Court was allowing itself to meddle in the internal affairs of a single state. The recount should continue. Their hue and cry failed to alter the results.

The Court's most tenacious supporters of the 'equal protection' stringent interpretation of the Constitution had corrupted their own principles. According to one opinion, "No one familiar with the jurisprudence of Justices Rehnquist, Scalia, and Thomas could possibly have imagined that they would vote to invalidate the Florida recount process on the basis of their own well-developed and oft-invoked approach to the Equal Protection Clause."

Later studies revealed that on the eve of the election Sandra Day O'Connor had made a public statement that a Gore victory would be a personal disaster for her. Clarence Thomas' wife was so intimately involved in the Bush campaign that she was helping to draw up a list of Bush appointees more or less at the same time as her husband was adjudicating on whether the same man would become the next President. Finally, Antonin Scalia's son was working for the firm appointed by Bush to argue his case before the Supreme Court, the head of which was subsequently appointed as Solicitor-General. The presumed impartiality of the nation's highest court had suffered a serious blow and George Bush became President with 271 electoral votes.

A young orphaned child had enflamed a community enough to elect a President who had lost the popular vote in the country by a half million votes and by one vote on the Supreme Court the United States would turn in a new direction.

EPILOGUE

Close votes will continue to dominate our elections and our court decisions. We are a divided nation. We come together in times of war and disasters but our attitudes on social mores and economic policies range across a broad spectrum. More and more, shouting drowns out political discourse and compromise.

In spring 2012 Supreme Court Chief Justice John Roberts cast the Court's deciding 5-4 vote in favor of the expansion of medical coverage to an additional 35 million Americans. His vote was totally unexpected, shocking all the political pundits. The effects of his decision will not be known for several years but, once again, a single vote altered the direction of our country.

In fall 2012 Barack Obama won reelection in a bitter and rancorous Presidential contest. He faces a divided Congress and it will be interesting to see if, once again, brave individuals step apart from the masses to cast a single vote that will move our country forward.

About the Author

Carole Eglash-Kosoff lives and writes in Valley Village, California. She graduated from UCLA and spent her career teaching, writing, and traveling to more than seventy countries. An avid student of history,  she researched the decades preceding and following the Civil War for nearly two years, including time in Louisiana, the setting for **Winds of Change** and her earlier novel, **When Stars Align**. They are both stories of mixed race love during a period of terrible injustice. They are stories of war, reconstruction, and racism, but most of all; they are stories of hope.

BY ONE VOTE is her 4th book. It deals with significant events in America's history. The concept of this book had been with her for several decades but it would take the evolution of the internet and her love of history to complete the research necessary.

In 2006, following the death of her husband, mother, and brother within a month, she spent several months teaching in the black townships of South Africa. Her first book, **The Human Spirit – Apartheid's Unheralded Heroes,** tells the true life stories of an amazing array of men and women who have devoted their lives during the worst years of apartheid to help the children, the elderly, and the disabled of the townships. These people cared when no one else did and their efforts continue to this day. Her second book, **When Stars Align**, was a well-received novel of mixed race lovers, Thaddeus, colored, born from the rape of a young slave girl by the scion of the plantation, Moss Grove. His love for Amy, white, carries them both through the Civil War and Reconstruction but their stars never align.

Winds of Change, released in late 2011, follows the characters of **When Stars Align** into the decades that closed out one century and led us into the next, decades that saw the introduction of the automobile, the airplane, and the telephone as well as the Spanish-American War, and World War I.

Acknowledgments

I am fortunate to have a wonderful cadre of professionals and friends who have taken the time to read and comment on this book. I want to thank Lauren Silinsky, Linda Martin, and Arleen Tisherman for their efforts and encouragement. A special thanks goes to Morgan Sloane and Michael Borden for their work in producing a demo reel of the book for television. Thanks, also, to Jon Jackson for his computer magic and technical skills

Carole Eglash-Kosoff

Email: ceglash@aol.com

Other Books By Carole Eglash-Kosoff:

THE HUMAN SPIRIT
~ Apartheid's Unheralded Heroes

ISBN-10: 1452033064
ISBN-13: 978-1452033068

240 Pages 6" x 9"

More information is available on the
website:www.thehumanspirit-thebook.com
or scan here

Prologue

Apartheid in South Africa has now been
gone more than fifteen years but the heroes
of their struggle to achieve a Black
majority-run democracy are still being
revealed. Some individuals toiled publicly, but most
worked tirelessly in the shadows to improve the welfare of
the Black and Colored populations that had been so
neglected. Nelson Mandela was still in prison; clean water
and sanitation barely existed; AIDS was beginning to
orphan an entire generation.

Meanwhile a white, Jewish, middle class woman, joined
with Tutu, Millie, Ivy, Zora and other concerned Black
women, respectfully called Mamas, to help those most in
need, often being beaten and arrested by white security
police.

This book tells the story of these women and others who
have spent their adult lives making South Africa a better
place for those who were the country's most
disadvantaged.

When Stars Align

ISBN-10: 1456738909

ISBN-13: 978-1456738907

412 Pages 6″ x 9″

Also Available: Hard Cover & Kindle

More information is available on the website:

www.whenstarsalign-thebook.com

or **scan here**

Prologue

The love that Thaddeus and Amy feel for one another can get them both killed.   He is colored, an ex-slave, and she is white. In 19th century Louisiana mixed race relationships are both illegal and unacceptable.

Moss Grove, a large Mississippi River cotton plantation has thrived from the use of slave labor while its owners lived lives of comfort and privilege. Thaddeus, born more than a decade earlier from the rape of a young field slave by the heir to the plantation, is raised as a Moss Grove house servant.   His presence remains a thorn in the side of the man who sired him.

Deepening divisiveness between North and South launches the Civil War and changes Moss Grove in ways no one could have anticipated.   With the war swirling we see the battles and carnage through Thaddeus' eyes. The war ends and he returns to Moss Grove and to Amy, hoping to enjoy their newly won freedoms. With the help of Union soldiers, schools are established to educate those who were formerly prohibited from learning to read. Medical clinics are opened and businesses begun. Black legislators are elected and help to pass new laws. Hope flourishes. Perhaps the stars will now finally align for the young lovers.

In 1876, however, the ex-Confederate states barter the selection of President Rutherford B. Hayes for removal of all Union troops from their soil in the most contested election in American history. Within a decade hopes are dashed as Jim Crow laws are passed, the Ku Klux Klan launches new violence, and black progress is crushed.

'When Stars Align' is a soaring novel of memorable white, Negro, and colored men and women set against actual

historic events.

Winds Of Change

ISBN#978-0-9839601-0-2 (Softback)

ISBN#978-0-9839601-1-9 (eBook)

More information is available on the website:

www.windsofchange-thebook.com

or scan here

Prologue

The racially charged love and conflict of the critically acclaimed *When Stars Align* become more entrenched after the Civil War and Reconstruction. Amy had taken her daughter, nephew, and a son she'd never been able to acknowledge, born from her love with Thaddeus, her colored lover, to San Francisco, as a refuge from the intense racial scrutiny of the South.

They are forced to return to their old home, Moss Grove, a successful Mississippi River cotton plantation, as young adults. They discover facts about themselves that refute everything they believed regarding both their parents and their racial background. It changes the lives of each of them. Bess and Stephen's love is thwarted. Josiah struggles with echoes of his past.

It is a tumultuous time in American history that includes the inventions of airplanes, automobiles, telephones and movies midst decades of lynching's and economic turmoil. It is the Spanish-American War and World War I. Racial biases complicate lives and relationships as newly arrived immigrants vie with white and Negro workers all trying to gain a piece of the American dream. **Winds of Change** is a soaring historic fiction novel that stands alone but follows the next generation from those we came to know in *When Stars Align into the 20th century*. It is a socially relevant, historically accurate, saga of decades often overlooked in American history.

CPSIA information can be obtained at www.ICGtesting.com
Printed in the USA
BVOW040746040213

312320BV00001B/4/P